New Baby Knits

New Baby Knits

More than 30
patterns for
0~3 year olds

Debbie Bliss

ST. MARTIN'S GRIFFIN ☙ *NEW YORK*

This book is dedicated to my mother.

**Library of Congress Cataloguing-in-
Publication Date**
  Bliss, Debbie:
  New Baby Knits: Debbie Bliss
  ISBN 0-312-07397-6
  1. Knitting Patterns 2. Children's
  clothing 3. Sweaters
  I Title
  TY825. B566   1991
746.9'2-dc20   91-17757
                  CIP

First published in Great Britain by Ebury Press
First St. Martin's Griffin Edition December 1996

10 9 8 7 6 5 4 3 2 1

Designed by Jerry Goldie
Photography by Sandra Lousada
Styling by Marie Willey

Printed and bound in Italy by New Interlitho,
S.p.a, Milan

Also by Debbie Bliss

Baby Knits
Kids' Country Knits
Kids' Knits for Heads, Hands & Toes
Toy Knits
Nursery Knits

Contents

Introduction

I am delighted to have been given the opportunity to present another collection of designs for 0–3 year-olds. As with my first book, *Baby Knits*, my aim has been to combine style with comfort and wearability, and the designs cover a range of knitting skills, with a combination of simple knits in basic stitches to more complicated patterns.

I have designed all the garments to have a fairly generous fit, but as actual measurements are included in the patterns, readers can select the size they prefer. All the yarns used are machine washable and where suitable I have quoted both pure wool and wool mix yarns.

The styles range from new-look Arans and delicate Fair Isles to tapestry effects and nursery motifs, and I have also included variations on some favourites from *Baby Knits*.

Debbie Bliss

Basic Information

Yarns

All yarn amounts are based on average requirements and should therefore be regarded as approximate. Use only the yarn specified: we cannot be responsible for an imperfect garment if any other brand is used.

Tension/stitch gauge

The flow of yarn which is controlled by the knitter is known as tension/stitch gauge, and is as personal as handwriting. Some knitters put more stress on the yarn, making a smaller stitch and tighter knitted fabric; others put less stress on the yarn and make a looser fabric. For this reason a tension sample is essential for the success of your finished garment.

You must always measure the tension/stitch gauge before you start to make anything. This is necessary for two reasons: to check your tension/stitch gauge against the measurements given in a pattern, and to calculate the number of stitches to cast on and rows to work when you are planning a design of your own. The tension/stitch gauge is always given at the beginning of a pattern and states the number of stitches and rows to the centimetre or inch using the yarn, needles and stitch pattern for a given design.

Calculating the number of stitches and rows is known as tension/stitch gauging. Three factors influence this:
1 The size of needles and type of yarn.
2 The type of stitch pattern.
3 The knitter.

Making a tension/stitch gauge sample

Use the same yarn, needles and stitch pattern as those to be used for the main work. Knit a sample at least 12.5 × 12.5 cm/5 × 5 in square. Smooth out the finished sample on a flat surface but do not stretch it.

Measuring the number of stitches

This determines the width of the knitting. Place a steel ruler or tape measure across the sample and mark 10 cm/ 4 in across with pins. Count the number of stitches between the pins. For complete accuracy, pin out the sample several times. An extra half stitch will prove to be vital when you are working from a knitting pattern or when you are gauging the number of stitches to cast on for your own design.

Adjusting tension/stitch gauge

The tension/stitch gauge can be adjusted by changing the size of needles and working another sample. If there are too many stitches to the centimetre or to the inch, your tension/stitch gauge is too tight and you should change to needles a size larger. If there are too few stitches, your tension/stitch gauge is too loose and you should change to needles a size smaller. If the number of stitches is correct but the number of rows incorrect, check the length as you proceed with the pattern.

Measuring the number of rows

This determines the depth of the knitting. The tension/ stitch gauge also determines the number of rows to the centimetre or to the inch. Place a ruler vertically along the fabric and mark out 10 cm/4 in with pins. Count the number of rows between the pins. From this count you can gauge the number of rows needed to reach the planned length of a design. You can also calculate where shaping is required and the position of increases and decreases.

Garment care

A knitted garment will have a much longer life and better appearance if it is properly cared for. Always look on the ball band and check instructions for cleaning and pressing. Where the garment should be handwashed, wash in lukewarm water using a soap especially designed for knitwear. Do not leave to soak, immerse garment and squeeze it gently, avoiding wringing or rubbing. Rinse thoroughly in tepid water, then gently squeeze to remove all excess water. Hold the garment at all times otherwise the weight will pull it out of shape. Place a towel on a table and dry the garment flat, patting it into shape. Dry away from direct heat.

Note

Figures for larger sizes are given in ( ) brackets. Where only one set of figures appears, this applies to all sizes. Work figures given in [ ] brackets the number of times stated afterwards. Where the figure 0 appears no stitches or rows are worked for this size.

*Aran Sweater
with Triangle Welt
and Collar*

SEE PAGE
39

*Guernsey
Sweater with
Fair Isle Bands
and Beret*

SEE PAGE
40

Cross-Over Cardigan

SEE PAGE
41

*Garter Stitch
with Shoes*

SEE PAGE
43

Striped Sweater with Zig Zag Collar and Bootees

SEE PAGE
44

*Fair Isle
Cardigan
with Beret*

SEE PAGE
45

Fair Isle Sweater with Hat

SEE PAGE
46

*Scandinavian
Cardigan,
Hat and Boots*
SEE PAGE
48

Cardigan with Lace Edgings

SEE PAGE
49

*Long Line Fair Isle
Sweater with Pockets
and Socks*

SEE PAGE
50

All In One

SEE PAGE
52

*Chick Cardigan
and Bootees*

SEE PAGE
54

Classic Jacket

SEE PAGE
55

Peasant Style Cardigan

SEE PAGE
56

Navajo Jacket
SEE PAGE
58

Folkloric Cardigan

SEE PAGE
60

Hooded Fair Isle Jacket

SEE PAGE
62

Tyrolean Cardigan

SEE PAGE
63

*Farmyard
Cardigan*

SEE PAGE
64

Aran
Sweater Dress
SEE PAGE
66

*Aran Coat
With Large Collar*

SEE PAGE
67

Nursery Sweater

SEE PAGE
70

Mexican Jacket

SEE PAGE
69

Duck Sweater and Pants

SEE PAGE
73

*Bee Cardigan
and Bootees
and Beanie Hat*

SEE PAGE
74

*Fisherman's Rib
Cardigan with
Saddle Shoulders*

SEE PAGE
76

*Fisherman's Rib
Sweater with
Saddle Shoulders*

SEE PAGE
75

Aran Jackets
SEE PAGE
76

Guernsey Style
Sweater
SEE PAGE
78
Crochet Hat
SEE PAGE
79

Aran Sweater with Triangle Welt and Collar

SEE PAGE
8

MATERIALS
8 (9) 50g balls of Hayfield Pure Wool Classics DK or 6 (7) 50g balls of Hayfield Grampian DK.
1 pair each of 3¼ mm (No 10/US 3) and 4 mm (No 8/US 5) knitting needles.
Cable needle.

MEASUREMENTS
To fit age   1–2 (2–3) years
All round at chest
              68 (73) cm   26¾ (28¾) in
Length to shoulder
              38 (43) cm   15 (17) in
Sleeve seam 20 (24) cm   8 (9½) in

TENSION
22 sts and 28 rows to 10 cm/4 in over st st on 4 mm (No 8/US 5) needles.

ABBREVIATIONS
Cr 4L = slip next 2 sts onto cable needle and leave at front, P2, then K2 from cable needle.
Cr 4R = slip next 2 sts onto cable needle and leave at back, K2, then P2 from cable needle.
CF   = slip next 2 sts onto cable needle and leave at front, P1, then K2 from cable needle.
CB   = slip next st onto cable needle and leave at back, K2, then P1 from cable needle.
C4B = slip next 2 sts onto cable needle and leave at back, K2, then K2 from cable needle.
C4F = slip next 2 sts onto cable needle and leave at front, K2, then K2 from cable needle.
MK   = (Make Knot) [K1, P1, K1, P1, K1, P1, K1] all in next st, then with point of left-hand needle, pass 2nd, 3rd, 4th, 5th, 6th and 7th sts over 1st st.
Also see box on this page.

Panel A – worked over 12 sts.
1st row (wrong side) K2, P2, K4, P2, K2.
2nd row P2, K2, P4, K2, P2.
3rd and every foll alt row K the K sts and P the P sts as they appear.
4th row P2, Cr 4L, Cr 4R, P2.
6th row P4, Cr 4L, P4.
8th row P6, CF, P3.
10th row P7, CF, P2.
12th row P3, MK, P4, K2, P2.
14th row P7, CB, P2.
16th row P6, CB, P3.
18th row P4, C4B, P4.
20th row P2, Cr 4R, Cr 4L, P2.
22nd row As 2nd row.
24th row As 4th row.
26th row P4, Cr 4R, P4.
28th row P3, CB, P6.
30th row P2, CB, P7.
32nd row P2, K2, P4, MK, P3.

34th row P2, CF, P7.
36th row P3, CF, P6.
38th row P4, C4F, P4.
40th row As 20th row.
These 40 rows form patt.

Panel B – worked over 10 sts.
1st row (wrong side) K1, P8, K1.
2nd row P1, K8, P1.
3rd and 2 foll alt rows As 1st row.
4th row P1, C4B, C4F, P1.
6th row As 2nd row.
8th row P1, C4F, C4B, P1.
These 8 rows form patt.

Panel C – worked over 20 sts.
1st row (wrong side) [K3, P2] twice, [P2, K3] twice.
2nd row [P2, CB] twice, [CF, P2] twice.
3rd row and every foll alt row K the K sts and P the P sts as they appear.
4th row P1, [CB, P2] twice, CF, P2, CF, P1.
6th row [CB, P2] twice, pick up loop between sts and [K1, P1, K1] into it, turn, P3, turn, slip 1, K2 tog, psso, P1, then pass the bobble st over this st, P1, CF, P2, CF.
8th row [CF, P2] twice, [P2, CB] twice.
10th row P1, [CF, P2] twice, CB, P2, CB, P1.
12th row [P2, CF] twice, [CB, P2] twice.
These 12 rows form patt.

Panel D – worked over 12 sts.
1st row (wrong side) K2, P2, K4, P2, K2.
2nd row P2, K2, P4, K2, P2.
3rd row and every foll alt row K the K sts and P the P sts as they appear.
4th row P2, Cr 4L, Cr 4R, P2.
6th row P4, Cr 4R, P4.
8th row P3, CB, P6.
10th row P2, CB, P7.
12th row P2, K2, P4, MK, P3.
14th row P2, CF, P7.
16th row P3, CF, P6.
18th row P4, C4F, P4.
20th row P2, Cr 4R, Cr 4L, P2.
22nd row As 2nd row.
24th row As 4th row.
26th row P4, Cr 4L, P4.
28th row P6, CF, P3.
30th row P7, CF, P2.
32nd row P3, MK, P4, K2, P2.
34th row P7, CB, P2.
36th row P6, CB, P3.
38th row P4, C4B, P4.
40th row As 20th row.
These 40 rows form patt.

Back
With 4 mm (No 8/US 5) needles, cast on 102 (110) sts.
Work in patt as follows:
1st row (wrong side) K1, [P1, K1] 3(5) times, work 1st row of Panel A, *K1, P4, K1, work 1st row of Panel B, K1, P4, K1*, work 1st work of Panel C, rep from * to * once,

work 1st row of Panel D, K1, [P1, K1] 3 (5) times.
2nd row P1, [K1, P1] 3 (5) times, work 2nd row of Panel D, *P1, K4, P1, work 2nd row of Panel B, P1, K4, P1*, work 2nd row of Panel C, rep from * to * once, work 2nd row of Panel A, P1, [K1, P1] 3 (5) times.
3rd row P1, [K1, P1] 3 (5) times, work 3rd row of Panel A, *K1, P4, K1, work 3rd row of Panel B, K1, P4, K1*, work 3rd row of Panel C, rep from * to * once, work 3rd row of Panel D, P1, [K1, P1] 3 (5) times.
4th row K1, [P1, K1] 3 (5) times, work 4th row of Panel D, P1, C4B, P1, work 4th row of Panel B, P1, C4B, P1, work 4th row of Panel C, P1, C4F, P1, work 4th row of Panel B, P1, C4F, P1, work 4th row of Panel A, K1, [P1, K1] 3 (5) times.
These 4 rows set patt. Cont in patt as set, working appropriate rows of Panels until work measures 35 (40) cm/13¾ (15¾) in from beg, ending with a wrong side row.
Shape shoulders
Cast off 16 (17) sts at beg of next 2 rows and 16 (18) sts at beg of foll 2 rows. Leave rem 38 (40) sts on a holder.

Front
Work as given for Back until work measures 29 (34) cm/11½ (13½) in from beg, ending with a wrong side row.
Shape neck
Next row Patt 39 (42), turn.
Work on this set of sts only.
Dec one st at neck edge on every row until 32 (35) sts rem.
Cont without shaping until work measures same as Back to shoulder shaping, ending at side edge.
Shape shoulder
Cast off 16 (17) sts at beg of next row. Patt 1 row. Cast off rem 16 (18) sts.

Continued overleaf

With right side facing, slip centre 24 (26) sts onto a holder, rejoin yarn to rem sts and patt to end. Complete to match first side.

Sleeves

With 3¼ mm (No 10/US 3) needles, cast on 40 (44) sts. Work in K1, P1 rib for 3 cm/ 1¼ in.

Next row Rib 0 (2), [inc in each of next 3 sts, rib 1] to last 0 (2) sts, rib 0 (2). 70 (74) sts. Change to 4 mm (No 8/US 5) needles. Work in patt as follows:

1st row (wrong side) K1, [P1, K1] 4 (5) times, work 1st row of Panel B, K1, P4, K1, work 1st row of Panel C, K1, P4, K1, work 1st row of Panel B, K1, [P1, K1] 4 (5) times.

2nd row P1, [K1, P1] 4 (5) times, work 2nd row of Panel B, P1, K4, P1, work 2nd row of Panel C, P1, K4, P1, work 2nd row of Panel B, P1, [K1, P1] 4 (5) times.

3rd row P1, [K1, P1] 4 (5) times, work 3rd row of Panel B, K1, P4, K1, work 3rd row of Panel C, K1, P4, K1, work 3rd row of Panel B, P1, [K1, P1] 4 (5) times.

4th row K1, [P1, K1] 4 (5) times, work 4th row of Panel B, P1, C4B, P1, work 4th row of Panel C, P1, C4F, P1, work 4th row of Panel B, K1, [P1, K1] 4 (5) times.

These 4 rows set patt. Cont in patt as set, working appropriate rows of Panels, *at the same time,* inc one st at each end of next and 2 foll 2nd (3rd) rows, then on every foll 3rd row until there are 94 (102) sts, working inc sts into double moss st (side edge) patt. Cont without shaping until work measures 20 (24) cm/8 (9½) in from beg, ending with a wrong side row. Cast off.

Collar

Join right shoulder seam. With 3¼ mm (No 10/US 3) needles and right side facing, pick up and K 23 sts down left front neck, K across 24 (26) sts at centre front, dec 4 (2) sts evenly, pick up and K 23 sts up right front neck and K across 38 (40) sts on back neck, dec 6 (2) sts evenly. 98 (108) sts. Work 7 rows in K1, P1 rib, inc one st at centre of last row on 1st size only. 99 (108) sts. K 3 rows.

*Next row (right side) K9, turn. Work on these sts only.

Next row K2 tog tbl, K5, K2 tog.
Next row K3, MK, K3.
Next row K2 tog tbl, K3, K2 tog.
Next row K5.
Next row K2 tog tbl, K1, K2 tog.
Next row K3.
Next row Sl 1, K2 tog, psso. Fasten off.
With right side facing, rejoin yarn to rem sts. Rep from * until all sts are worked off.

Welt Edgings

With 3¼ mm (No 10/US 3) needles and right side facing, pick up and K 81 (90) sts evenly along cast on edge of Back. K 3 rows. Now work as given for collar from * until all sts are worked off.
Work front edging in same way.

To Make Up

Join left shoulder seam and rib section of collar.
Sew on sleeves, placing centre of sleeves to shoulder seams.
Join side and sleeve seams.

Guernsey Sweater with Fair Isle Bands and Beret

SEE PAGE
9

MATERIALS

Sweater : 3 (4) × 50g balls of Hayfield Grampian DK in main colour (M).
Small amounts of same in 3 colours (A, B and C).
1 pair each of 3¼ mm (No 10/US 3) and 4 mm (No 8/US 5) knitting needles. Cable needle. 3 buttons.

Beret : 1 × 50g ball of Hayfield Grampian DK in main colour (M).
Small amount of same in 3 colours (A, B and C).
1 pair of 3¾ mm (No 9/US 4) knitting needles.

MEASUREMENTS

To fit age   6 (12) months
All round at chest
                    57 (64) cm   22½ (25) in
Length to shoulder
                    28 (33) cm   11 (13) in
Sleeve seam   16 (22) cm   6¼ (8½) in

TENSION

22 sts and 28 rows to 10 cm/4 in over st st on 4 mm (No 8/US 5) needles.

ABBREVIATIONS

See page 39.

NOTE

Strand yarn not in use loosely across wrong side to keep fabric elastic when working Fair Isle.

Panel A – worked over 13 sts.
1st row (right side) K13.

2nd row P13.
3rd row K6, P1, K6.
4th row P5, K3, P5.
5th row K4, P2, K1, P2, K4.
6th row P3 [K2, P3] twice.
7th row K2, P2, K5, P2, K2.
8th row P1, K2, P7, K2, P1.
9th row As 7th row.
10th row As 6th row.
11th row As 5th row.
12th row As 4th row.
13th row As 3rd row.
14th row P13.
Rep 3rd to 14th rows for patt.

Panel B – worked over 11 sts.
1st row (right side) K1, P2, K8.
2nd row P7, K2, P2.
3rd row K3, P2, K6.
4th row P5, K2, P4.
5th row K5, P2, K4.
6th row P3, K2, P6.
7th row K7, P2, K2.
8th row P1, K2, P8.
9th row K8, P2, K1.
10th row P2, K2, P7.
11th row K6, P2, K3.
12th row P4, K2, P5.
13th row K4, P2, K5.
14th row P6, K2, P3.
15th row K2, P2, K7.
16th row P8, K2, P1.
These 16 rows form patt.

Panel C – worked over 11 sts.
1st row (right side) K11.
2nd row P11.

3rd to 10th rows Work 1st to 8th rows of Panel B.
These 10 rows form patt.

Panel D – worked over 8 sts.
1st row (right side) P2, K4, P2.
2nd row K2, P4, K2.
3rd row P2, slip next 2 sts onto cable needle and leave at front, K2, then K2 from cable needle, P2.
4th row As 2nd row.
5th and 6th rows As 1st and 2nd rows.
These 6 rows form patt.

Panel E – worked over 13 sts.
1st row (right side) K13.
2nd row P13.
3rd row K6, P1, K6.
4th row P5, K1, P1, K1, P5.
5th row K4, P1, [K1, P1] twice, K4.
6th row P3, K1, [P1, K1] 3 times, P3.
7th row K2, P1, [K1, P1] 4 times, K2.
8th row P1, [K1, P1] 6 times.
9th row As 7th row.
10th row As 6th row.
11th row As 5th row.
12th row As 4th row.
13th row As 3rd row.
14th row P13.
These 14 rows form patt.

Panel F – worked over 11 sts.
1st row (right side) K11.
2nd row P11.
3rd to 10th rows Work 9th to 16th rows of Panel B.
These 10 rows form patt.

Sweater

Back

With 3¼ mm (No 10/US 3) needles and M, cast on 66 (74) sts.

1st row (right side) K2, [P2, K2] to end.
2nd row P2, [K2, P2] to end.

Rep last 2 rows until welt measures 3 cm/1¼ in from beg, ending with a wrong side row and inc 3 sts evenly across last row. 69 (77) sts.

Change to 4 mm (No 8/US 5) needles. Work in main patt as follows:

1st row (right side) K0 (2), P0 (3), K2 (1),* P3, K1, P3, work 1st row of Panel A, P3, K1, P3*, work 1st row of Panel B, rep from * to * once, K2 (1), P0 (3), K0 (2).
2nd row P0 (1), [P1, K1] 0 (2) times, P2 (1),* K1, [P1, K1] 3 times, work 2nd row of Panel A, K1, [P1, K1] 3 times*, work 2nd row of Panel B, rep from * to * once, P2 (1), [K1, P1] 0 (2) times, P0 (1).

These 2 rows set main patt. Cont in main patt as set, working appropriate rows of Panels until work measures 16 (18) cm/6¼ (7) in from beg, ending with a wrong side row. P 4 rows.

**Work Fair Isle border as follows:
1st row (right side) K1 B, [1M, 1A, 1M, 1B] to end.
2nd row P1 M, [1A, 1M] to end.
3rd row K1A, [1M, 1C, 1M, 1A] to end.
4th row As 2nd row.
5th row As 1st row.

Cont in M only, P 5 rows**. Work in yoke patt as follows:

1st row (right side) K1, [K1, P3] 2 (3) times, work 1st row of Panels C, D, E, D and F, [P3, K1] 2 (3) times, K1.
2nd row P1, [P1, K1] 4 (6) times, work 2nd row of Panels F, D, E, D and C, [K1, P1] 4 (6) times, P1.

These 2 rows set yoke patt. Cont in yoke patt as set, working appropriate rows of Panels until work measures 28 (33) cm/11 (13) in from beg, ending with a wrong side row.

Shape shoulders

Cast off 20 (23) sts at beg of next 2 rows. Leave rem 29 (31) sts on a holder.

Front

Work as given for Back until work measures 24 (28) cm/9½ (11) in from beg, ending with a wrong side row.

Shape neck

Next row Patt 28 (31), turn.

Work on this set of sts only. Keeping patt correct, dec one st at neck edge on every row until 20 (23) sts rem.

Cont without shaping for a few rows until work measures same as Back to shoulder shaping, ending at side edge. Cast off.

With right side facing, slip centre 13 (15) sts onto a holder, join yarn to rem sts and patt to end. Complete to match first side.

Sleeves

With 3¼ mm (No 10/US 3) needles and M, cast on 38 (42) sts.

Work in rib as given for Back for 3 cm/1¼ in, ending with a wrong side row and inc 13 (9) sts evenly across last row. 51 sts.

Change to 4 mm (No 8/US 5) needles. Work in main patt as follows:

1st row (right side) Work 1st row of Panel A, P3, K1, P3, work 1st row of Panel B, P3, K1, P3, work 1st row of Panel A.
2nd row Work 2nd row of Panel A, K1, [P1, K1] 3 times, work 2nd row of Panel B, K1, [P1, K1] 3 times, work 2nd row of Panel A.

These 2 rows set main patt. Cont in main patt, *at the same time* inc one st at each end of next and every foll 2nd (4th) row until there are 69 sts, working inc sts to match side edge patt on Back.

Cont without shaping until work measures 12 (18) cm/4¾ (7) in, ending with a wrong side row. P 4 rows. Now work as given for Back from ** to **. Cast off.

Neckband

Join right shoulder seam.

With 3¼ mm (No 10/US 3) needles, M and right side facing, pick up and K 18 sts down left front neck, K across 13 (15) sts at centre front, pick up and K 18 sts up right front neck, K across 29 (31) sts on back neck. 78 (82) sts. Beg with a 2nd row, work 8 rows in rib as given for Back. Cast off in rib.

Buttonhole Band

With 3¼ mm (No 10/US 3) needles, M and right side facing, pick up and K 30 (34) sts evenly across left front shoulder and neckband.

Beg with a 2nd row, work 3 rows in rib as given for Back.

1st buttonhole row Rib 4(5), [cast off 2, rib 7 (8) sts more] twice, cast off 2, rib to end.
2nd buttonhole row Rib to end, casting on 2 sts over those cast off in previous row. Rib 3 rows. Cast off in rib.

Button Band

Work to match buttonhole band, but picking up sts across left back shoulder and neckband and omitting buttonholes.

To Make Up

Lap buttonhole band over button band and catch down at side. Sew on sleeves, placing centre of right sleeve to shoulder seam and centre of left sleeve in line with buttonholes.

Join side and sleeve seams. Sew on buttons.

Beret

With 3¾ mm (No 9/US 4) needles and M, cast on 75 sts. K 5 rows.

Inc row K4, [M1, K1, M1, K10] 6 times, M1, K1, M1, K4. 89 sts.

Now work 1st to 5th rows of Fair Isle border as given for Back of Sweater.

P 1 row in M.

Cont in M only and garter st (every row K), work as follows:

Inc row K5, [M1, K1, M1, K12] 6 times, M1, K1, M1, K5. K 5 rows.
Inc row K6, [M1, K1, M1, K14] 6 times, M1, K1, M1, K6. K 5 rows.

Cont in this way inc 14 sts on next and every foll 6th row until there are 159 sts. K 4 rows.

Dec row K8, [K2 tog, K1, K2 tog, K18] 6 times, K2 tog, K1, K2 tog, K8. K 4 rows.
Dec row K7, [K2 tog, K1, K2 tog, K16] 6 times, K2 tog, K1, K2 tog, K7. K 4 rows.
Dec row K6, [K2 tog, K1, K2 tog, K14] 6 times, K2 tog, K1, K2 tog, K6.

Cont in this way, dec 14 sts on every 5th row until 33 sts rem. K 1 row.

Next 2 rows K1, [K2 tog] to end. 9 sts.

Break off yarn, thread end through rem sts, pull up, secure, then join seam.

Using all four colours, make a large pompon and attach to top of beret.

Cross-Over Cardigan

SEE PAGE
10

MATERIALS

2 × 50g balls of Hayfield Pure Wool Classics 4 ply in main colour (M).

1 × 50g ball of same in 8 contrast colours (A, B, C, D, E, F, G and H).

1 pair each of 2¾ mm (No 12/US 1), 3 mm (No 11/US 2) and 3¼ mm (No 10/US 3) knitting needles.

MEASUREMENTS

To fit age
12–18 (18–24:24–36) months
All round at chest
49 (53:56) cm   19¼ (21:22) in
Length to shoulder
29 (33:36) cm   11½ (13:14) in
Sleeve seam
19 (22:26) cm   7½ (8½:10¼) in

TENSION

32 sts and 32 rows to 10 cm/4 in over patt on 3¼ mm (No 10/US 3) needles.

ABBREVIATIONS

See page 39.

continued overleaf

NOTE

When working in patt, strand yarn not in use loosely across wrong side to keep fabric elastic.

Back

With 2¾ mm (No 12/US 1) needles and M, cast on 73 (79:85) sts.
1st row (right side) K1, [P1, K1] to end.
2nd row P1, [K1, P1] to end.
Rep these 2 rows until work measures 4 cm/1½ in from beg, ending with a wrong side row and inc 6 sts evenly across last row. 79 (85:91) sts.
Change to 3¼ mm (No 10/US 3) needles. Beg with a K row and working in st st throughout, work patt from chart as indicated for Back, reading K rows from right to left and P rows from left to right until work measures 18 (21:23) cm/7 (8¼:9) in from beg, ending with a wrong side row.
Shape armholes
Cast off 9 sts at beg of next 2 rows. 61 (67:73) sts.
Keeping patt correct, cont without shaping until work measures 29 (33:36) cm/11½ (13:14) in from beg, ending with a wrong side row.
Shape shoulders
Cast off 8 (9:10) sts at beg of next 4 rows. Cast off rem 29 (31:33) sts.

Left Front

With 2¾ mm (No 12/US 1) needles and M, cast on 67 (73:79) sts.
Work in rib as given for Back for 4 cm/1½ in, ending with a wrong side row and inc 6 sts evenly across last row. 73 (79:85) sts.
Change to 3¼ mm (No 10/US 3) needles. Beg with a K row and working in st st throughout, work patt from chart as indicated for Left Front for 4 (6:6) rows.
Shape front
Keeping patt correct, dec one st at end (front edge) of next row and at beg of foll row, then work 1 row straight. Cont dec one st at front edge on next 2 rows, then work 1 row straight until 49 (59:69) sts rem, ending with a dec row. Now dec one st at front edge on every foll alt row until work measures 18 (21:23) cm/7 (8¼:9) in from beg, ending with a wrong side row.
Shape armhole
Cont to dec at front edge as before, cast off 9 sts at beg of next row.
Keeping armhole edge straight, cont to dec at front edge as before until 16 (18:20) sts rem.
Cont without shaping, until work measures same as Back to shoulder shaping, ending with a wrong side row.
Shape shoulder
Cast off 8 (9:10) sts at beg of next row.
Work 1 row. Cast off rem 8 (9:10) sts.

Right Front

Work as given for Left Front, following chart as indicated for Right Front and reversing all shaping.

Sleeves

With 2¾ mm (No 12/US 1) needles and M,
cast on 39 (41:41) sts.
Work in rib as given for Back for 4 cm/1½ in, ending with a wrong side row and inc 4 (8:14) sts evenly across last row. 43 (49:55) sts.
Change to 3¼ mm (No 10/US 3) needles. Beg with a K row and working in st st throughout, work in patt from chart as indicated for Back, *at the same time*, inc one st at each end of every foll 4th (5th:6th) row until there are 61 (67:73) sts, working inc sts into patt.
Cont without shaping until work measures 22 (25:29) cm/8¾ (10:11½) in from beg, ending with a wrong side row.
Shape top
Cast off 5 sts at beg of next 10 rows. Cast off rem 11 (17:23) sts.

Front Band

With 3 mm (No 11/US 2) needles and M, cast on 7 sts. Work in garter st (every row K) until band, when slightly stretched, fits up along front edge of Right Front, across back neck and down front edge of Left Front. Cast off.

Ties (make 2)

With 3 mm (No 11/US 2) needles and M, cast on 7 sts.
Work in garter st until work measures 25 (28:31) cm/10 (11:12) in.
Cast off.

To Make Up

Join shoulder seams. Sew on front band. Sew on sleeves, sewing last 3 cm/1¼ in of row ends before top shaping to cast off sts at armholes.
Join sleeve and side seams, leaving 2 cm/¾ in opening above welt at right side seam.
Sew cast on edges of ties above welts to each front.

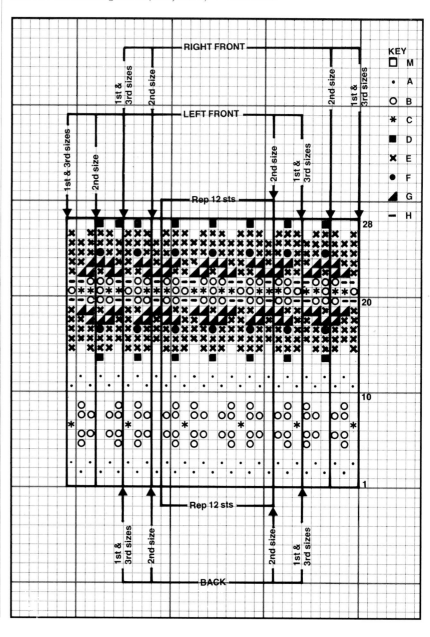

Garter Stitch Jacket with Shoes

SEE PAGE 11

MATERIALS

Jacket : 4 (4:5) 50g balls of Hayfield Grampian DK in main colour (M).
Small amount of same in contrast colour (A).
Oddments in each of 2 contrast colours (B and C) for embroidery.
1 pair each of 3¼ mm (No 10/US 3) and 4 mm (No 8/US 5) knitting needles.
2 buttons.

Shoes : 1 × 50g ball of Hayfield Grampian 4 ply in contrast colour (A).
Oddments in each of 2 contrast colours (B and C) for embroidery.
1 pair of 3 mm (No 11/US 2) knitting needles.
2 buttons.

MEASUREMENTS

To fit age
6–12 (12–24:24–36) months
All round at chest
60 (66:70) cm   23½ (26:27½) in
Length to shoulder
27 (33:38) cm   10½ (13:15) in
Sleeve seam
16 (21:24) cm   6¼ (8¼:9½) in

TENSION

22 sts and 44 rows to 10 cm/4 in over garter stitch (every row K) on 4 mm (No 8/US 5) needles using DK yarn.

ABBREVIATIONS

See page 00.

Jacket

Back

With 4 mm (No 8/US 5) needles and A, cast on 67 (73:77) sts. K 4 rows, thus ending with a wrong side row.
Change to M and cont in garter st until work measures 16 (20:24) cm/6¼ (8:9½) in from beg, ending with a wrong side row.
Shape armholes
Cast off 4 (5:5) sts at beg of next 2 rows. 59 (63:67) sts.
Cont without shaping until work measures 27 (33:38) cm/10½ (13:15) in from beg, ending with a wrong side row.
Shape shoulders
Cast off 8 (8:9) sts at beg of next 2 rows and 8 (9:9) sts at beg of foll 2 rows. Leave rem 27 (29:31) sts on a holder.

Pocket Linings (Make 2)

With 4 mm (No 8/US 5) needles and M, cast on 15 (17:17) sts. K 20 (22:22) rows. Leave these sts on a spare needle.

Left Front

With 4 mm (No 8/US 5) needles and A, cast on 31 (35:37) sts. K 4 rows, thus ending with a wrong side row.
Change to M. K 20 (22:22) rows.
Place pocket
Next row K9 (10:11), slip next 15 (17:17) sts onto a holder, K across 15 (17:17) sts of one pocket lining, K to end.
Cont in garter st across all sts until work measures same as Back to armhole shaping, ending with a wrong side row.
Shape armhole
Cast off 4 (5:5) sts at beg of next row. 27 (30:32) sts.
Cont without shaping until work measures 24 (29:34) cm/9½ (11½:13½) in from beg, ending with a right side row.
Shape neck
Cast off 4 (4:5) sts at beg of next row.
Dec one st at neck edge on every row until 16 (17:18) sts rem.
Cont without shaping until work measures same as Back to shoulder shaping, ending with a wrong side row.
Shape shoulder
Cast off 8 (8:9) sts at beg of next row.
Work 1 row. Cast off rem 8 (9:9) sts.

Right Front

Work as given for Left Front, reversing all shaping and placing pocket as follows:
Next row K7 (8:9), slip next 15 (17:17) sts onto a holder, K across 15 (17:17) sts of one pocket lining, K to end.

Sleeves

With 4 mm (No 8/US 5) needles and A, cast on 34 (40:44) sts. K 4 rows, thus ending with a wrong side row.
Change to M and cont in garter st, inc one st at each end of every 6th (7th:8th) row until there are 54 (62:66) sts.
Cont without shaping until work measures 18 (23:26) cm/7 (9:10¼) in, ending with a wrong side row. Cast off.

Pocket Tops

With 3¼ mm (No 10/US 3) needles, right side facing and A, K across sts of one pocket top inc one st at centre. 16 (18:18) sts. K 4 rows. Cast off knitwise.

Right Front Band

With 3¼ mm (No 10/US 3) needles, right side facing and A, pick up and K 43 (52:63) sts evenly along front edge of Right Front, picking up and P sts from wrong side over last 5 cm/2 in. K 4 rows. Cast off knitwise.

Left Front Band

Work to match Right Front Band, picking up and P sts from wrong side over first 5 cm/2 in.

Neckband

Join shoulder seams. With 3¼ mm (No 10/US 3) needles, right side facing and A, pick up and K 21 (23:23) sts up right front neck, picking up and P sts from wrong side over first 3 cm/1¼ in, K across 27 (29:31) sts at back neck, pick up and K 21 (23:23) sts down left front neck, picking up and P sts from wrong side over last 3 cm/1¼ in. 69 (75:77) sts. K 4 rows. Cast off knitwise.

To Make Up

With B and C embroider flowers and leaves in lazy daisy st with French Knot (see diagram page 61) in centre on pockets and at centre of lower edge of sleeves as shown.
Catch down pocket linings and sides of pocket tops. Sew in sleeves, gathering slightly at top and sewing last 2 cm/1¾ in of row ends of sleeve tops to cast off sts at armholes.
Join side and sleeve seams. Turn top corners of fronts over for lapels and sew buttons to each through both thicknesses.

Shoes

With 3 mm (No 11/US 2) needles and A, cast on 13 sts for top.
K 20 rows, thus ending with a wrong side row. Leave these sts.
With 3 mm (No 11/US 2) needles and A, cast on 17 sts, then with right side facing pick up and K14 sts along right row end edge of top, K13 sts across, then pick up and K14 sts along other side of top, turn and cast on 17 sts. 75 sts.
K 11 rows.
Shape sole
1st row Slip 1, K32, K2 tog, K5, K2 tog, K to end.
2nd row Slip 1, K31, K2 tog, K5, K2 tog, K to end.
3rd row Slip 1, K2, K2 tog, K24, K2 tog, K3, K3 tog, K3, K2 tog, K24, K2 tog, K3.
4th and 5th rows Slip 1, K to end.
6th row K2 tog, [K3, K2 tog, K22, K2 tog] twice, K3, K2 tog.
7th and 8th rows Slip 1, K to end.
9th row K2 tog, K2, K2 tog, K18, [K2 tog, K1] 4 times, K17, K2 tog, K2, K2 tog.
10th row Slip 1, K to end.
11th row Slip 1, [K2 tog, K1] 3 times, K10, [K2 tog, K1] 4 times, K10, [K2 tog, K1] 3 times. 41 sts. Cast off.
With 3 mm (No 11/US 2) needles and A, cast on 45 sts for strap. K 2 rows.
Buttonhole row K3, yf, K2 tog, K to end. K 1 row. Cast off knitwise.
Join back and sole seam. Place centre of strap to back seam of shoe and sew 1.5 cm/½ in each side of seam. Sew on button. With B and C, embroider flower in lazy daisy stitch with French Knot (see diagram page 75) in centre on top of shoe as shown.
Make another shoe in same way, reversing buttonhole row.

Striped Sweater with Zig Zag Collar and Bootees

SEE PAGE
12

MATERIALS

Sweater : 2 (2:3) balls of Hayfield Pure Wool Classics 4 ply in each of 2 colours (A and B).
Bootees : 1 ball of Hayfield Pure Wool Classics 4 ply in each of 2 colours (A and B).
1 pair each of 2¾ mm (No 12/US 1) and 3¼ mm (No 10/US 3) knitting needles.
2 buttons for Sweater and 2 buttons for Bootees.

MEASUREMENTS

To fit age
    3 (6:9) months
All round at chest
    54 (56:58) cm   21¼ (22:23) in
Length to shoulder
    24 (27:30) cm   9½ (10½:11¾) in
Sleeve seam
    15 (17:19) cm   6 (6¾:7½) in

TENSION

28 sts and 36 rows to 10 cm/4 in over st st on 3¼ mm (No 10/US 3) needles.

ABBREVIATIONS

See page 39.

Sweater

Back

With 2¾ mm (No 12/US 1) needles and A, cast on 75 (79:83) sts.
1st row (right side) K1, [P1, K1] to end.
2nd row P1, [K1, P1] to end.
Rep these 2 rows until work measures 3 cm/1¼ in from beg, ending with a wrong side row.
Change to 3¼ mm (No 10/US 3) needles.
Beg with a K row and working in st st and stripe patt of 2 rows B, 2 rows A throughout, cont until work measures 13 (15:17) cm/5 (6:6¾) in from beg, ending with a wrong side row.
Shape armholes
Cast off 4 sts at beg of next 2 rows. 67 (71:75) sts.
Cont without shaping until work measures 24 (27:30) cm/9½ (10½:11¾) in from beg, ending with a wrong side row.
Shape shoulders
Cast off 9 (9:10) sts at beg of next 2 rows and 9 (10:10) sts at beg of foll 2 rows. Cast off rem 31 (33:35) sts.

Front

Work as given for Back until work measures 13 (15:17) cm/5 (6:6¾) in from beg, ending with a wrong side row.
Shape armholes and divide for front opening
Next row Cast off 4, K until there are 31 (33:35) sts on right hand needle, cast off next 5 sts, K to end.

Work on last set of 35 (37:39) sts only. Cast off 4 sts at beg of next row. 31 (33:35) sts.
Cont without shaping until work measures 19 (22:25) cm/7½ (8¾:10) in from beg, ending at inside edge.
Shape neck
Cast off 4 (4:5) sts at beg of next row and 2 (3:3) sts at beg of foll alt row. Dec one st at neck edge on next 5 rows, then on 2 foll alt rows. 18 (19:20) sts.
Cont without shaping until work measures same as Back to shoulder shaping, ending at armhole edge.
Shape shoulder
Cast off 9 (9:10) sts at beg of next row. Work 1 row. Cast off rem 9 (10:10) sts.
With wrong side facing, rejoin yarn to rem sts and complete to match first side.

Sleeves

With 2¾ mm (No 12/US 1) needles and A, cast on 37 (39:41) sts.
Work in rib as given for Back for 3 cm/1¼ in, ending with a right side row.
Next row Rib 5 (5:4), [M1, rib 2, M1, rib 1] to last 5 (4:4) sts, M1, rib to end. 56 (60:64) sts.
Change to 3¼ mm (No 10/US 3) needles.
Work in st st and stripe patt as given for Back, *at the same time*, inc one st at each end of every 9th row until there are 62 (68:74) sts.
Cont without shaping until work measures 16 (18:20) cm/6¼ (7:8) in from beg, ending with a wrong side row. Cast off.

Collar

Join shoulder seams.
With 2¾ mm (No 12/US 1) needles, B and right side facing, pick up and K22 (22:24) sts up right front neck, 33 (33:36) sts across back neck and 22 (22:24) sts down left front neck. 77 (77:84) sts. K 3 rows.
Next row Rib 1 (1:2), M1, [rib 2, M1, rib 3, M1] to last 1 (1:2) sts, rib to end. 108 (108:117) sts.
K 12 rows.
*1st row (right side) K9, turn. Work on these 9 sts only.
2nd row K2 tog tbl, K5, K2 tog.
3rd row K7.
4th row K2 tog tbl, K3, K2 tog.
5th row K5.
6th row K2 tog tbl, K1, K2 tog.
7th row K3.
8th row Slip 1, K2 tog, psso and fasten off.
With right side facing, rejoin yarn to rem sts.
Rep from * until all sts are worked off.

Button Band

With 2¾ mm (No 12/US 1) needles, B and right side facing, pick up and K 18 (18:20) sts evenly along left side edge of front opening, omitting collar. K 12 rows. Cast off.

Buttonhole Band

With 2¾ mm (No 12/US 1) needles, B and right side facing, pick up and K 18 (18:20) sts evenly along right side edge of front opening, omitting collar. K 5 rows, dec one st at each end of last row on 3rd size only.
1st row K9, turn. Work on these 9 sts only.
2nd row (buttonhole) K2 tog tbl, K2, yf, K2 tog, K1, K2 tog.
Now work 3rd to 8th rows of collar.** With right side facing, rejoin yarn to rem sts. Rep from ** to ** once more.

To Make Up

Sew on sleeves, placing centre of sleeves to shoulder seams. Join side and sleeve seams. Sew on buttons.

Bootees

With 3¼ mm (No 10/US 3) needles and A, cast on 40 sts. K 1 row.
Cont in st st and stripe patt of 2 rows B, 2 rows A throughout, work as follows:
Next row Inc in first st, P18, inc in each of next 2 sts, P18, inc in last st. Work 1 row.
Next row Inc in first st, P20, inc in each of next 2 sts, P20, inc in last st. Work 1 row.
Next row Inc in first st, P22, inc in each of next 2 sts, P22, inc in last st. 52 sts. Work 6 rows.
Shape instep
Next row K30, slip 1, K1, psso, turn.
Next row P9, P2 tog, turn.
Next row K9, slip 1, K1, psso, turn.
Rep last 2 rows 4 times more, then the 1st of the 2 rows again.
Next row K to end. 40 sts. Work 2 rows across all sts.
Shape back heel
Next row P8, turn. Work 7 rows on these 8 sts. Leave these sts on a spare needle.
With wrong side facing, slip next 24 sts onto a holder, join yarn to rem 8 sts and work 8 rows.
Next row P to end then P across 8 sts of other side of back heel. 16 sts.
Cont in A only.
Next row Cast on 22 sts, P to end.
Buttonhole row K to last 3 sts, yf, K2 tog, K1. P 1 row. Cast off.
With 2¾ mm (No 12/US 1) needles, A and right side facing, pick up and K 8 sts down inside edge of back heel, K across 24 sts on a holder, pick up and K 8 sts up inside edge of back heel. 40 sts. Cast off knitwise.
With 2¾ mm (No 12/US 1) needles and B, cast on 45 sts for edging. K 4 rows.
Now rep from * as given for Collar of Sweater until all sts are worked off.
Join back heel and sole seam. Sew on edging to strap. Sew on button.

Make another bootee, reversing strap.

Fair Isle Cardigan with Beret

SEE PAGE
13

MATERIALS

Sweater : 1 (1:1:2) 50g balls of Hayfield Pure Wool Classics 4 ply in main colour (M).

1 × 50g ball of same in 8 contrast colours (A, B, C, D, E, F, G and H).

1 pair each of 2¾ mm (No 12/US 1) and 3¼ mm (No 10/US 3) knitting needles.

4 buttons.

Beret : Small amounts of Hayfield Pure Wool Classics 4 ply in 9 colours (M, A, B, C, D, E, F, G and H).

Set of four 2¾ mm (No 12/US 1) and 3¼ mm (No 10/US 3) double pointed knitting needles.

MEASUREMENTS

To fit age

6–9 (12:24:36) months

All round at chest

56 (61:67:72) cm   22 (24:26½:28½) in

Length to shoulder

27 (31:35:39) cm 10½ (12¼:13¾:15¼) in

Sleeve seam

18 (21:24:27) cm   7 (8¼:9½:10½) in

TENSION

32 sts and 32 rows to 10 cm/4 in over patt on 3¼ mm (No 10/US 3) needles.

ABBREVIATIONS

See page 39.

NOTE

When working in patt, strand yarn not in use loosely across wrong side to keep fabric elastic.

Sweater

Back

With 2¾ mm (No 12/US 1) needles and M, cast on 81 (87:93:99) sts.

1st row (right side) K1, [P1, K1] to end.

2nd row P1, [K1, P1] to end.

Rep these 2 rows until work measures 4 cm/1½ in from beg, ending with a right side row.

Next row Rib 4 (5:7:4), [inc in next st, rib 7 (6:5:5) sts] to last 5 (5:8:5) sts, inc in next st, rib to end. 91 (99:107:115) sts.

Change to 3¼ mm (No 10/US 3) needles. Beg with a K row and working in st st throughout, work in patt from chart 1 as indicated for Back, reading K rows from right to left and P rows from left to right until work measures 27 (31:35:39) cm/10½ (12¼:13¾:15¼) in from beg, ending with a wrong side row.

Shape shoulders

Cast off 15 (16:17:18) sts at beg of next 4 rows. Leave rem 31 (35:39:43) sts on a holder.

Left Front

With 2¾ mm (No 12/US 1) needles and M, cast on 37 (41:43:47) sts.

Work in rib as given for Back for 4 cm/ 1½ in, ending with a right side row.

Next row Rib 3 (5:4:2), [inc in next st, rib 5 (5:4:5) sts] to last 4 (6:4:3) sts, inc in next st, rib to end. 43 (47:51:55) sts.

Change to 3¼ mm (No 10/US 3) needles.

Beg with a K row and working in st st throughout, work in patt from chart 1 as indicated for Left Front until work measures 17 (19:21:23) cm/6¾ (7½:8¼:9) in from beg, ending with a wrong side row.

Shape front

Dec one st at end (front edge) of next and every foll alt row until 30 (32:34:36) sts rem. Cont without shaping until work measures same as Back to shoulder shaping, ending with a wrong side row.

Shape shoulder

Cast off 15 (16:17:18) sts at beg of next row. Work 1 row.

Cast off rem 15 (16:17:18) sts.

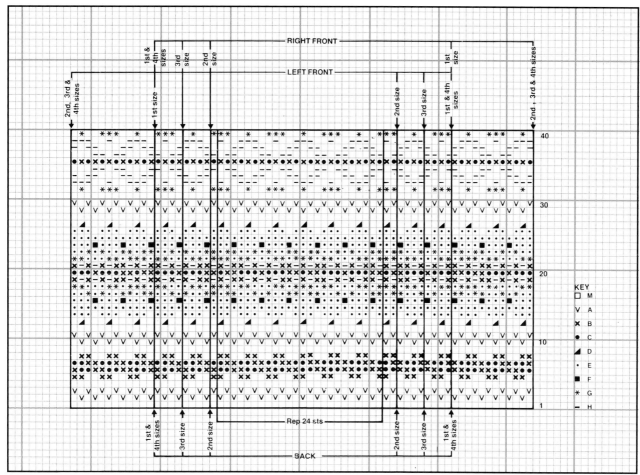

continued overleaf

Right Front

Work as given for Left Front, following chart 1 as indicated for Right Front and reversing all shaping.

Sleeves

With 2¾ mm (No 12/US 1) needles and M, cast on 49 (51:53:55) sts.
Work in rib as given for Back for 4 cm/1½ in, ending with a wrong side row and inc 2 (8:6:12) sts evenly across last row. 51 (59:59:67) sts.
Change to 3¼ mm (No 10/US 3) needles. Beg with a K row and working in st st throughout, work in patt from chart 1 as indicated for 2nd (3rd:3rd:4th) sizes on Back, *at the same time*, inc one st at each end of every foll 2nd (3rd:3rd:5th) row until there are 79 (83:87:91) sts, working inc sts into patt.
Cont without shaping until work measures 18 (21:24:27) cm/7 (8¼:9½:10½) in from beg, ending with a wrong side row.
Cast off.

Front Band

Join shoulder seams.
With 2¾ mm (No 12/US 1) needles, M and right side facing, pick up and K 53 (59:65:71) sts evenly along straight edge of Right Front, 31 (37:43:49) sts along shaped edge to shoulder, K across 31 (35:39:43) sts on back neck, pick up and K 31 (37:43:49) sts along shaped edge of Left Front and 53 (59:65:71) sts down straight edge. 199 (227:255:283) sts.
Work 3 rows in rib as given for Back.
1st buttonhole row Rib 3, [cast off 2, rib 13 (15:17:19) sts more] 4 times, rib to end.
2nd buttonhole row Rib to end, casting on 2 sts over those cast off in previous row.
Rib 3 rows. Cast off in rib.

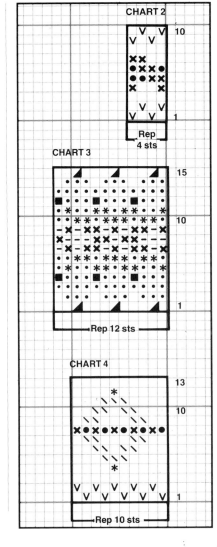

CHART 2

Rep 4 sts

CHART 3

Rep 12 sts

CHART 4

Rep 10 sts

To Make Up

Sew on sleeves, placing centre of sleeves to shoulder seams.
Join side and sleeve seams. Sew on buttons.

Beret

With set of four 2¾ mm (No 12/US 1) needles and M, cast on 92 (102:112:122) sts. Work 7 rounds in K1, P1 rib.
Next round *Rib 1 (2:3:4), [inc in each of next 3 sts, rib 1] 11 (12:13:14) times, inc in next st; rep from * once more. 160 (176: 192:208) sts.
Change to set of four 3¼ mm (No 10/US 3) needles.
Work in st st (every round K) throughout and patt from charts (read every row of chart from right to left) as follows:
Work 10 rounds from chart 2.
With M, work 2 (3:5:5) rounds, dec 4 sts evenly across last round on 1st and 4th sizes only and inc 4 sts evenly across last round on 2nd size only. 156 (180:192: 204) sts.
Now work 15 rounds from chart 3.
With M, work 1 (2:3:4) rounds.
Dec round [K4, K2 tog] to end. 130 (150:160:170) sts.
Work 13 rounds from chart 4.
Dec round *[K1M, 1A] twice, with M, K3 tog, K1A, 1M, 1A; rep from * to end.
Dec round [K1A, 1M, 1A, with M, K3 tog, K1A, 1M] to end.
Cont in M only.
Dec round [K2, K3 tog, K1] to end.
Dec round [K1, K3 tog] to end.
Dec round [K2 tog] to end. 13 (15:16:17) sts.
Break off yarn, thread end through rem sts, pull up and secure.

Fair Isle Sweater with Hat

SEE PAGE 14

MATERIALS

Sweater : 2 (2:3) 50g balls of Hayfield Grampian DK in main colour (A).
1 ball of same in each of 4 colours (B, C, D and E).
1 pair each of 3¼ mm (No 10/US 3) and 4 mm (No 8/US 5) knitting needles.
Set of four 3¼ mm (No 10/US 3) double pointed knitting needles.
Hat : 1 × 50g ball of Hayfield Grampian DK in main colour (A).
Small amounts of same in each of 4 colours (B, C, D and E).
Set of four 4 mm (No 8/US 5) double pointed knitting needles.

MEASUREMENTS

To fit age
　　1 (2:3) years
All round at chest
　　60 (68:76) cm　　23½ (26¾:30) in
Length to shoulder
　　30 (33:37) cm　　11¾ (13:14½) in
Sleeve seam
　　22 (25:28) cm　　8¾ (10:11) in

TENSION

24 sts and 24 rows to 10 cm/4 in over patt on 4 mm (No 8/US 5) needles.

ABBREVIATIONS

See page 39.

NOTE

Strand yarn not in use loosely across wrong side to keep fabric elastic.

Sweater

Back

With 3¼ mm (No 10/US 3) needles and A, cast on 65 (75:83) sts.
1st row (right side) K1, [P1, K1] to end.
2nd row P1, [K1, P1] to end.
Rep these 2 rows until work measures 5 cm/2 in from beg, ending with a wrong side row and inc 8 sts evenly across last row. 73 (83:91) sts.
Change to 4 mm (No 8/US 5) needles.
Beg with a K row and working in st st throughout, cont in patt from chart 1 as indicated for Back, reading K rows from right to left and P rows from left to right until work measures 30 (33:37) cm/11¾ (13: 14½) in from beg, ending with a wrong side row.

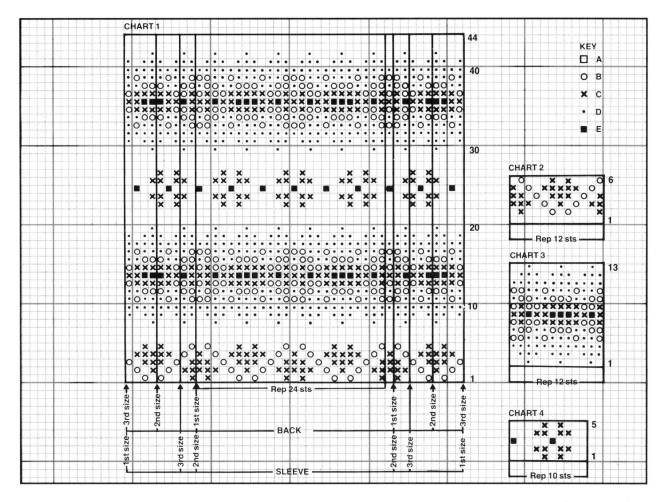

CHART 1

CHART 2
Rep 12 sts

CHART 3
Rep 12 sts

CHART 4
Rep 10 sts

KEY
☐ A
O B
✕ C
• D
■ E

Rep 24 sts

BACK

SLEEVE

Shape shoulders
Cast off 11 (13:14) sts at beg of next 4 rows.
Leave rem 29 (31:35) sts on a holder.

Front
Work as given for Back until work measures 24 (27:31) cm/9½ (10½:12) in from beg, ending with a wrong side row.
Shape neck
Next row Patt 29 (33:36), turn.
Work on this set of sts only. Keeping patt correct, dec one st at neck edge on every row until 22 (26:28) sts rem.
Cont without shaping until work measures same as Back to shoulder shaping, ending at side edge.
Shape shoulder
Cast off 11 (13:14) sts at beg of next row.
Work 1 row. Cast off rem 11 (13:14) sts.
With right side facing, slip centre 15 (17:19) sts onto a holder, rejoin yarn to rem sts and patt to end. Complete to match first side.

Sleeves
With 3¼ mm (No 10/US 3) needles and A, cast on 33 (37:41) sts.
Work in rib as given for Back for 5 cm/2 in, ending with a wrong side row and inc 10 (12:12) sts evenly across last row. 43 (49:53) sts.
Change to 4 mm (No 8/US 5) needles.
Beg with a K row and working in st st throughout, cont in patt from chart 1 as

indicated for Sleeve, *at the same time,* inc one st at each end of every 2nd (3rd:3rd) row until there are 71 (75:79) sts, working inc sts into patt.
Cont without shaping until work measures 22 (25:28) cm/8¾ (10:11) in from beg, ending with a wrong side row. Cast off.

Collar
Join shoulder seams.
With set of four 3¼ mm (No 10/US 3) needles, A and right side facing, slip first 8 (9:10) sts from holder at centre front onto a safety pin, join yarn to next st and K rem 7 (8:9) sts, pick up and K 16 sts up right front neck, K across 29 (31:35) sts on back neck, pick up and K 16 sts down left front neck then K sts from safety pin. 76 (80:86) sts.
Work in rounds of K1, P1 rib for 2 cm/¾ in, dec one st at end of last round.
Turn and cont backwards and forwards as follows:
Next round Rib 3, work 3 times in next st, rib to last 4 sts, work 3 times in next st, rib 3. Rib 1 row.
Rep last 2 rows until collar measures 8 (8:9) cm/3 (3:3½) in from beg. Cast off loosely.

To Make Up
Sew on sleeves, placing centre of sleeves to shoulder seams. Join side and sleeve seams.

Hat

With set of four 4 mm (No 8/US 5) needles and A, cast on 80 (88:96) sts.
Work 8 rounds in K1, P1 rib.
Next round *[Inc in each of next 5 sts, rib 1] 3 (3:1) times, [inc in next st, rib 1] 1 (2:1) times; rep from * to end. 144 (156:168) sts.
Cont in st st (every round K) throughout, reading every row of chart from right to left, work 6 rounds from chart 2, then work 2 (3:4) rounds in A. Now work 13 rounds from chart 3, then work 1 (2:3) rounds in A.
Next round With A, [K4, K3 tog, K5] to end. 120 (130:140) sts.
Work 5 rounds from chart 4.
Shape crown
Next round With A, [K3, K3 tog, K4] to end. With A, K1 round.
Next round [With A, K2, K3 tog, K2, with D, K1] to end.
Next round [K1D, with A, K3 tog, with D, K2] to end.
Next round [With D, K3 tog, K1] to end.
Next round [With D, K2 tog] to end. 12 (13:14) sts.
Break off yarn, thread end through rem sts, pull up and secure.

Sport weight

Scandinavian Cardigan, Hat and Boots

SEE PAGE
15

MATERIALS
Cardigan : 3 (4) 50g balls of Hayfield
Pure Wool Classics DK or 3 × 50g balls of
Hayfield Grampian DK in main colour (M).
1 (2) balls of same in contrast colour (A).
1 pair each of 3¼ mm (No 10/US 3) and
4 mm (No 8/US 5) knitting needles.
5 (6) buttons.
Hat : 1 × 50g ball of Hayfield Pure Wool
Classics DK or Hayfield Grampian DK in
main colour (M).
1 ball of same in contrast colour (A).
Oddment of Red for pompons.
1 pair each of 3¼ mm (No 10/US 3) and
4 mm (No 8/US 5) knitting needles.
Boots : 1 × 50g ball of Hayfield Pure Wool
Classics 4 ply or Hayfield Grampian 4 ply in
main colour (M).
Oddment of Red for pompons.
1 pair of 2¾ mm (No 12/US 1) knitting
needles.

MEASUREMENTS
To fit age
    6–9 (9–12) months
All round at chest
    65 (71) cm   25½ (28) in
Length to shoulder
    27 (32) cm   10½ (12½) in
Sleeve seam
    18 (22) cm   7 (8¾) in

TENSION
24 sts and 25 rows to 10 cm/4 in over patt
on 4 mm (No 8/US 5) needles using DK
yarn.

ABBREVIATIONS
See page 39.

NOTE
When working motifs, use a separate
length of yarn for each section and twist
yarns together on wrong side when changing colour to avoid holes.
When working Fair Isle bands, strand yarn
not in use loosely across wrong side to
keep fabric elastic.

Cardigan

Back
With 3¼ mm (No 10/US 3) needles and M,
cast on 69 (75) sts.
1st row (right side) K1, [P1, K1] to end.
2nd row P1, [K1, P1] to end.
Rep these 2 rows until work measures
3 cm/1¼ in from beg, ending with a wrong
side row and inc 6 sts evenly across last
row. 75 (81) sts.
Change to 4 mm (No 8/US 5) needles.
Beg with a K row and working in st st

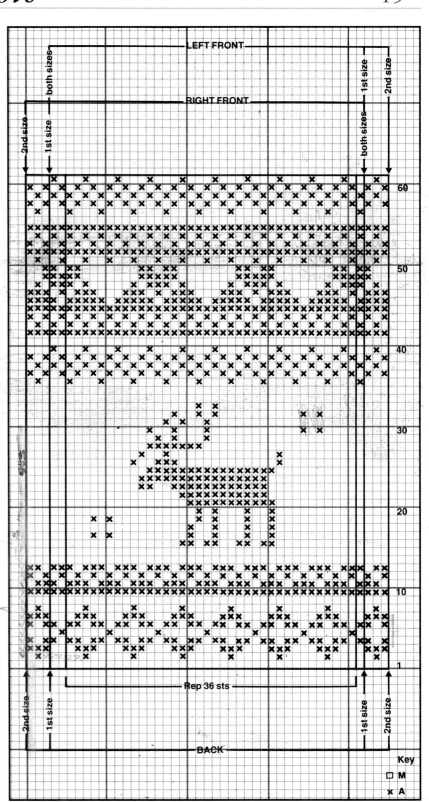

throughout, cont in patt from chart as indicated for Back, reading K rows from right to left and P rows from left to right, until work measures 27 (32) cm/10½ (12½) in from beg, ending with a wrong side row.

Shape shoulders

Cast off 21 (23) sts at beg of next 2 rows. Leave rem 33 (35) sts on a holder.

Left Front

With 3¼ mm (No 10/US 3) needles and M, cast on 37 (39) sts. Work in rib as given for Back for 3 cm/1¼ in, ending with a wrong side row and inc 2 (3) sts evenly across last row. 39 (42) sts.
Change to 4 mm (No 8/US 5) needles.
Beg with a K row and working in st st throughout, cont in patt from chart as indicated for Left Front until work measures 21 (26) cm/8¼ (10¼) in from beg, ending with a right side row.

Shape neck

Keeping patt correct, cast off 6 sts at beg of next row and 4 (5) sts at beg of foll alt row.
Dec one st at neck edge on every row until 21 (23) sts rem.
Cont without shaping for a few rows until work measures same as Back to shoulder shaping, ending with a wrong side row. Cast off.

Right Front

Work as given for Left Front, reversing all shaping and working patt from chart as indicated for Right Front.

Sleeves

With 3¼ mm (No 10/US 3) needles and M, cast on 41 sts. Work in rib as given for Back for 3 cm/1¼ in, ending with a wrong side row and inc 4 sts evenly across last row. 45 sts.
Change to 4 mm (No 8/US 5) needles.
Beg with a K row and working in st st throughout, cont in patt from chart as indicated for 2nd size on Back, *at the same time*, inc one st at each end of every foll alt row until there are 73 (77) sts, working inc sts into patt.
Cont without shaping until work measures 18 (22) cm/7 (8¾) in from beg, ending with a wrong side row. Cast off.

Neckband

Join shoulder seams.
With 3¼ mm (No 10/US 3) needles, M and right side facing, pick up and K 26 sts up right front neck, K across 33 (35) sts on back neck, pick up and K 26 sts down left front neck. 85 (87) sts.
Beg with a 2nd row, work in rib as given for Back for 3 cm/1¼ in. Cast off in rib.

Buttonhole Band

With 3¼ mm (No 10/US 3) needles, M and right side facing, pick up and K 61 (73) sts along Right Front to top of neckband. Beg with a 2nd row, work 3 rows in rib as given for Back.
1st buttonhole row Rib 3, [cast off 2, rib 10 sts more] 4 (5) times, cast off 2, rib to end.

2nd buttonhole row Rib to end, casting on 2 sts over those cast off in previous row. Rib 4 rows. Cast off in rib.

Button Band

Work to match Buttonhole Band, omitting buttonholes.

To Make Up

Sew on sleeves, placing centre of sleeves to shoulder seams. Join side and sleeve seams. Sew on buttons.

Hat

With 3¼ mm (No 10/US 3) needles and M, cast on 45 sts.
Work in rib as given for Back of Cardigan for 2 cm/¾ in, ending with a wrong side row.
Change to 4 mm (No 8/US 5) needles.
Beg with a K row and working in st st throughout, work 15th to 55th row of patt from chart as indicated for 2nd size on Back. Cast off.
Make another piece in same way. Join top and side seams. Make 2 pompons in Red and attach to each corner of hat.

Boots

Using M only, work as Sheep Boots to **.
Make pompon and attach to top of boot.
Make another boot in same way.

Cardigan with Lace Edgings

SEE PAGE 16

MATERIALS

4 (5:6) 50g balls of Hayfield Silky Cotton DK.
1 pair each of 3¼ mm (No 10/US 3) and 4 mm (No 8/US 5) knitting needles.
5 buttons.

MEASUREMENTS

To fit age
    1 (2:3) years
All round at chest
    60 (65:71) cm   23½ (25½:28) in
Length to shoulder
    30 (32:34) cm   12 (12½:13¼) in
Sleeve seam
    19 (21:24) cm   7½ (8¼:9½) in

TENSION

22 sts and 28 rows to 10 cm/4 in over st st on 4 mm (No 8/US 5) needles.

ABBREVIATIONS

See page 39.

Back

With 4 mm (No 8/US 5) needles, cast on 67 (73:79) sts.
Beg with a K row, work in st st until work measures 15 (16:17) cm/6 (6¼:6¾) in from beg, ending with a P row.

Shape armholes

Cast off 5 (6:7) sts at beg of next 2 rows.
Dec one st at each end of next 3 rows and 2 foll alt rows. 47 (51:55) sts.
Cont without shaping until work measures 28 (30:32) cm/11 (12:12½) in from beg, ending with a K row.

Shape neck

Next row P13 (14:15), cast off next 21 (23:25) sts, P to end.
Work on last set of sts only.

Shape shoulder

Cast off 6 (6:7) sts at beg of next row, 2 sts at beg of foll row. Cast off rem 5 (6:6) sts.
With right side facing, rejoin yarn to rem sts, K to end. Complete to match first side.

Left Front

With 4 mm (No 8/US 5) needles, cast on 31 (34:37) sts.
Beg with a K row, work in st st until work measures 15 (16:17) cm/6 (6¼:6¾) in from beg, ending with a P row.

Shape armhole and front edge

Cast off 5 (6:7) sts at beg of next row and 3 sts at beg (front edge) of foll row.
Dec one st at armhole edge on next 3 rows, then on 2 foll alt rows, *at the same time*, dec one st at front edge on foll 5th row.
Keeping armhole edge straight, dec one st at front edge on 3rd and every foll 4th row until 11 (12:13) sts rem.
Cont without spacing until work measures same as Back to shoulder shaping, ending with a P row.

Shape shoulder

Cast off 6 (6:7) sts at beg of next row. Work 1 row. Cast off rem 5 (6:6) sts.

Right Front

Work as given for Left Front, reversing all shaping.

Sleeves

With 4 mm (No 8/US 5) needles, cast on 35 (37:39) sts.
Beg with a K row, work in st st and inc one st at each end of every foll 5th row until there are 49 (53:57) sts.
Cont without shaping until work measures 17 (19:22) cm/6¾ (7½:8½) in from beg, ending with a P row.

Shape Top

Cast off 5 (6:7) sts at beg of next 2 rows.
Dec one st at each end of next and 1 (2:3) foll 4th rows, then on every alt row until 19 (21:19) sts rem.

continued overleaf

Now dec one st at each end of every row until 9 (11:13) sts rem. Cast off.

Button Band

With 3¼ mm (No 10/US 3) needles, cast on 6 sts.

Work in garter st (every row K) until band, when slightly stretched, fits up straight edge of Left Front. Cast off. Sew in place. Mark band to indicate buttons, first one to come 1 cm/¼ in up from cast on edge and last one 1 cm/¼ in down from cast off edge and rem 3 evenly spaced between.

Buttonhole Band

Work to match Button Band, working buttonholes at markers as follows:

1st buttonhole row (right side) K2, cast off 2, K to end.

2nd buttonhole row K2, cast on 2, K2.

Sew in place.

Collar

Join shoulder seams.

With 4 mm (No 8/US 5) needles, cast on 2 sts. K 1 row.

Next row Cast on 2, P to end. K 1 row.

Rep last 2 rows once. 6 sts.

Cont in st st, inc one st at beg (inside edge) of next and at same edge on 5 foll rows, then on every alt row until there are 21 sts. Now inc one st at inside edge on 3 foll 4th rows. 24 sts.

Cont without shaping for a few rows until collar fits shaped edge of Left Front to shoulder, ending with a P row.

Shape collar

1st row K5, turn.

2nd and every alt row Sl 1, P to end.

3rd row K10, turn.

5th row K15, turn.

7th row K20, turn.

9th row K24, turn.

11th row As 7th row.

13th row As 5th row.

15th row As 3rd row.

17th row As 1st row.

18th row As 2nd row.

Work across all sts until collar fits up shaped edge of Left Front to centre back neck. Complete other half of collar to match first half, but working decreases instead of increases.

Welt Edging

Join side seams.

With 3¼ mm (No 10/US 3) needles, cast on 4 sts. K 1 row.

1st row (wrong side) K2, yf, K2.

2nd row and 2 foll alt rows K.

3rd row K3, yf, K2.

5th row K2, yf, K2 tog, yf, K2.

7th row K3, yf, K2 tog, yf, K2.

8th row Cast off 4, K to end.

These 8 rows form patt. Cont in patt until edging, when slightly stretched, fits along cast on edges of Back, Fronts and Bands, ending with a 7th row. Cast off. Sew in place.

Sleeve Edgings

Work as given for Welt Edging, until edging when slightly stretched fits along cast on edge of Sleeves, ending with a 7th row. Cast off. Sew in place.

Collar Edging

Work as given for Welt Edging, until edging when slightly stretched fits up along straight outside edge of Collar, ending with a 7th row. Cast off.

To Make Up

Join sleeve seams. Set in sleeves. Sew collar edging in place, then sew on collar, beg and ending at centre of front bands. Sew on buttons.

Long Line Fair Isle Sweater with Pockets and Socks

SEE PAGE 17

MATERIALS

Sweater : 2 × 50g balls of Hayfield Pure Wool Classics 4 ply in main colour (M).

1 × 50g ball of same in 7 contrast colours (A, B, C, D, E, F and G).

1 pair each of 2¾ mm (No 12/US 1) and 3¼ mm (No 10/US 3) knitting needles.

Set of four 2¾ mm (No 12/US 1) double pointed knitting needles.

Socks : 1 × 50g ball of Hayfield Pure Wool Classics 4 ply in main colour (M).

Small amounts of same in 6 contrast colours (B, C, D, E, F and G).

1 pair each of 2¾ mm (No 12/US 1) and 3¼ mm (No 10/US 3) knitting needles.

Set of four 3¼ mm (No 10/US 3) double pointed knitting needles.

MEASUREMENTS

To fit age

9 (12:18) months

All round at chest

60 (64:70) cm   23½ (25¼:27½) in

Length to shoulder

32 (36:39) cm   12½ (14:15½) in

Sleeve seam

18 (21:24) cm   7 (8¼:9½) in

To fit foot

13 cm   5 in

Length to base of heel

13 cm   5 in

TENSION

32 sts and 32 rows to 10 cm/4 in over patt on 3¼ mm (No 10/US 3) needles.

ABBREVIATIONS

See page 39.

NOTE

When working in patt, strand yarn not in use loosely across wrong side to keep fabric elastic.

Sweater

Back

With 2¾ mm (No 12/US 1) needles and M, cast on 81 (85:93) sts.

1st row (right side) K1, [P1, K1] to end.

2nd row P1, [K1, P1] to end.

Rep these 2 rows until work measures 4 cm/1½ in from beg, ending with a right side row.

Next row Rib 1 (4:3), [inc in next st, rib 4 (3:3), inc in next st, rib 4] to end. 97 (103:113) sts.

Change to 3¼ mm (No 10/ US 3) needles. Beg with a K row and working in st st throughout, work patt from chart as indicated for Back, reading K rows from right to left and P rows from left to right until work measures 32 (36:39) cm/12½ (14:15½) in from beg, ending with a wrong side row.

Shape shoulders

Cast off 15 (16:18) sts at beg of next 4 rows.

Leave rem 37 (39:41) sts on a holder.

Pocket Linings (make 2)

With 3¼ mm (No 10/US 3) needles and M, cast on 26 sts. Work in st st until work measures 6 cm/2¼ in from beg, ending with a P row. Leave these sts on a holder.

Front

Work as given for Back until work measures 11 cm/4¼ in from beg, ending with a wrong side row.

Place pockets

Next row Patt 9 (10:11), *slip next 26 sts onto a holder, patt across sts of one pocket lining*, patt 27 (31:39), rep from * to * once, patt to end.

Cont in patt until work measures 27 (31:34) cm/10½ (12:13½) in from beg, ending with a wrong side row.

Shape neck

Next row Patt 39 (41:45), turn. Work on this set of sts only.

Keeping patt correct, dec one st at neck edge on every row until 30 (32:36) sts rem. Cont without shaping until work measures same as Back to shoulder shaping, ending

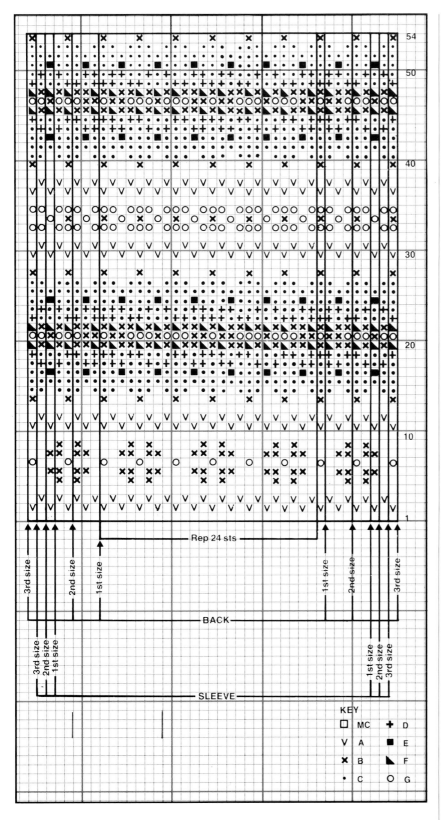

Rep 24 sts

3rd size
2nd size
1st size

BACK

1st size
2nd size
3rd size

3rd size
2nd size
1st size

1st size
2nd size
3rd size

SLEEVE

KEY

□	MC	+	D
V	A	■	E
✕	B	◣	F
•	C	O	G

with a wrong side row.
Shape shoulder
Cast off 15 (16:18) sts at beg of next row.
Patt 1 row. Cast off rem 15 (16:18) sts.
With right side facing, slip centre 19 (21:23)
sts onto a holder, rejoin yarn to rem sts and

patt to end. Complete to match first side,
reversing shaping.

Sleeves
With 2¾ mm (No 12/US 1) needles and M,
cast on 49 (51:53) sts.

Work in rib as given for Back for 4 cm/
1½ in, ending with a wrong side row and
inc 10 sts evenly across last row. 59 (61:63)
sts.
Change to 3¼ mm (No 10/US 3) needles.
Beg with a K row and working in st st
throughout, work in patt from chart as
indicated for Sleeve, *at the same time*, inc
one st at each end of every foll 3rd row until
there are 83 (89:95) sts, working inc sts into
patt.
Cont without shaping until work measures
18 (21:24) cm/7 (8¼:9½) in from beg,
ending with a wrong side row. Cast off.

Collar
Join shoulder seams.
With right side facing, slip first 9 (10:11) sts
from centre front holder onto a safety pin,
join M yarn to next st, and with set of four
2¾ mm (No 12/US 1) needles, K rem 10
(11:12) sts, pick up and K 18 sts up right
front neck, K across 37 (39:41) sts on back
neck inc 4 sts evenly, pick up and K 18 sts
down left front neck, then K9 (10:11) sts
from safety pin. 96 (100:104) sts.
Work in rounds of K1, P1 rib for 2 cm/¾ in,
inc one st at end of last round, turn. 97
(101:105) sts.
Work backwards and forwards in rib until
collar measures 6 (7:8) cm/2¼ (2¾:3) in.
Cast off loosely in rib.

Pocket Tops
With 2¾ mm (No 12/US 1) needles, M and
right side facing, K across sts on pocket
top, inc one st at centre. 27 sts.
Beg with a 2nd row, work 7 rows in rib as
given for Back. Cast off in rib.

To Make Up
Sew on sleeves, placing centre of sleeves
to shoulder seams. Join side and sleeve
seams. Catch down pocket linings and
sides of pocket tops.

Socks

With 2¾ mm (No 12/US 1) needles and M,
cast on 49 sts for cuff.
Work in rib as given for Back of Sweater for
4 rows.
Change to 3¼ mm (No 10/US 3) needles.
Beg with a K row and working in st st
throughout, work 13th to 29th rows of chart
as indicated for 1st size on Back, dec 6 sts
evenly across last row. 43 sts.
Cont in M only. Change to 2¾ mm (No 12/
US 1) needles.
Beg with a 1st row (thus reversing the
fabric), work in rib as given for Back of
Sweater until work measures 12 cm/4¾ in
from beg, ending with a wrong side row.
Change to 3¼ mm (No 10/US 3) needles.
Beg with a K row, work 4 rows in st st. Break
off yarn.
With set of four 3¼ mm (No 10/US 3)
needles, divide sts onto 3 needles as
follows:
Slip first 9 sts onto first needle, next 12 sts
onto second needle and next 12 sts onto

continued overleaf

third needle, slip last 10 sts onto other end of first needle.

Shape heel

With right side facing, join M yarn to 19 sts on first needle, K9, K2 tog, K8, turn. Work on these 18 sts only.

Beg with a P row, work 9 rows in st st.

Next row K13, K2 tog tbl, turn.

Next row Sl 1, P8, P2 tog, turn.

*Next row Sl 1, K8, K2 tog tbl, turn.

Next row Sl 1, P8, P2 tog, turn.*

Rep from * to * twice. 10 sts. Break off yarn.

Next round Reset sts on 3 needles as follows: Slip first 5 sts of heel sts onto a safety pin, place marker here to indicate beg of round, join M yarn to rem sts, with first needle K5, then pick up and K 8 sts along side of heel, K5, with second needle, K14, with 3rd needle K5, then pick up and K 8 sts along other side of heel, K5 from safety pin. 50 sts. K 1 round.

Next round K12, K2 tog, K to last 14 sts, K2 tog tbl, K12. K 1 round.

Next round K11, K2 tog, K to last 13 sts, K2 tog tbl, K11.

Cont in this way dec one st at each side of heel on every alt round until 40 sts rem. Cont without shaping until work measures 11 cm/4¼ in from back of heel.

Shape toe

Next round [K7, K2 tog, K2, K2 tog tbl, K7] twice. K 1 round.

Next round [K6, K2 tog, K2, K2 tog tbl, K6] twice.

Cont in this way dec 4 sts on every alt round until 20 sts rem. Divide sts onto 2 needles (sole and instep) and graft sts.

Join back seam, reversing seam on cuff to allow for turning.

All In One

SEE PAGE

18–19

MATERIALS

Lamb : 6 (7:8) 50g balls of Hayfield Pure Wool Classics DK in main colour (M).
1 ball of same in contrast colour (A).
Small amount of same in Dark Grey.

Bunny : 7 (8:9) 50g balls of Hayfield Pure Wool Classics DK in main colour (M).
Small amount of same in Pink.
Oddment of White mohair.
1 pair each of 3¼ mm (No 10/US 3) and 4 mm (No 8/US 5) knitting needles.
10 buttons.

MEASUREMENTS

To fit age
0–3 (3–6:6–9) months
All round at chest
53 (56:59) cm   21 (22:23¼) in
Length from beginning of leg to centre back neck
44 (48:52) cm   17¼ (19:20½) in
Inside leg seam
9 (11:13) cm   3½ (4¼:5) in
Sleeve seam
14 (16:18) cm   5½ (6¼:7) in

TENSION

22 sts and 44 rows to 10 cm/4 in over garter st (every row K) on 4 mm (No 8/US 5) needles.

ABBREVIATIONS

See page 39.

Lamb

Right Foot

With 4 mm (No 8/US 5) needles and A, cast on 32 (34:36) sts. K 1 row.

Next row K13 (14:15), M1, K1, M1, K15 (16:17), M1, K1, M1, K2.

K 1 row.

Next row K13 (14:15), M1, K3, M1, K15 (16:17), M1, K3, M1, K2.

K 1 row.

Next row K13 (14:15), M1, K5, M1, K15 (16:17), M1, K5, M1, K2.

K 1 row.

Next row K13 (14:15), M1, K7, M1, K15 (16:17), M1, K7, M1, K2.

K 1 row.

Next row K13 (14:15), M1, K9, M1, K15 (16:17), M1, K9, M1, K2. 52 (54:56) sts.

K 5 rows.

Next row K13 (14:15), K2 tog tbl, K7, K2 tog, K28 (29:30).

K 3 rows.

Next row K13 (14:15), K2 tog tbl, K5, K2 tog, K28 (29:30).

K 3 rows.

Next row K13 (14:15), K2 tog tbl, K3, K2 tog, K28 (29:30).

K 1 row.

Next row K12 (13:14), K2 tog, K3, K2 tog tbl, K27 (28:29).

K 1 row.

Next row K11 (12:13), K2 tog, K3, K2 tog tbl, K26 (27:28).

K 1 row.

Next row K10 (11:12), K2 tog, K3, K2 tog tbl, K25 (26:27).

K 1 row.

Next row K9 (10:11), K2 tog, K3, K2 tog tbl, K24 (25:26).

K 1 row.

Next row K8 (9:10), K2 tog, K3, K2 tog tbl, K23 (24:25). (36 (38:40) sts.

K 1 row. Change to M and K 1 row.

Work Right Leg as follows:

**Change to 3¼ mm (No 10/US 3) needles.

Next row (wrong side) *[K1, P1] twice, [K1, P1] all in next st; rep from * to last 1 (3:5) sts, [K1, P1] 0 (1:2) times, K1. 43 (45:47) sts.

Next row P1, [K1, P1] to end.

Next row K1, [P1, K1] to end.

Work a further 3 rows in rib.

Next row Rib 3 (3:2), [M1, rib 1, M1, rib 2] 13 (13:14) times, [M1, rib 2] 0 (1:1) time, rib 1. 69 (72:76) sts.

Change to 4 mm (No 8/US 5) needles and cont in garter st until work measures 9 (11:13) cm/3½ (4¼:5) in from beg of rib, ending with a wrong side row.

Shape crotch

Cast off 3 sts at beg of next 2 rows.

Dec one st at beg of next 4 rows.

K 1 row.**

Leave rem 59 (62:66) sts on a holder.

Left Foot

With 4 mm (No 8/US 5) needles and A, cast on 32 (34:36) sts. K 1 row.

Next row K2, M1, K1, M1, K15 (16:17), M1, K1, M1, K13 (14:15).

K 1 row.

Next row K2, M1, K3, M1, K15 (16:17), M1, K3, M1, K13 (14:15).

K 1 row.

Next row K2, M1, K5, M1, K15 (16:17), M1, K5, M1, K13 (14:15).

K 1 row.

Next row K2, M1, K7, M1, K15 (16:17), M1, K7, M1, K13 (14:15).

K 1 row.

Next row K2, M1, K9, M1, K15 (16:17), M1, K9, M1, K13 (14:15). 52 (54:56) sts.

K 5 rows.

Next row K28 (29:30), K2 tog tbl, K7, K2 tog, K13 (14:15).

K 3 rows.

Next row K28 (29:30), K2 tog tbl, K5, K2 tog, K13 (14:15).

K 3 rows.

Next row K28 (29:30), K2 tog tbl, K3, K2 tog, K13 (14:15).

K 1 row.

Next row K27 (28:29), K2 tog, K3, K2 tog tbl, K12 (13:14).

K 1 row.

Next row K26 (27:28), K2 tog, K3, K2 tog tbl, K11 (12:13).

K 1 row.

Next row K25 (26:27), K2 tog, K3, K2 tog tbl, K10 (11:12).

K 1 row.

Next row K24 (25:26), K2 tog, K3, K2 tog tbl, K9 (10:11).

K 1 row.

Next row K23 (24:25), K2 tog, K3, K2 tog tbl, K8 (9:10). 36 (38:40) sts.

K 1 row. Change to M and K 1 row.

Now work Left Leg as given for Right Leg, from ** to **.

Next row (wrong side) K to end, then K across sts of Right Leg. 118 (124:132) sts.

Work a further 3 cm/1¼ in in garter st, ending with a wrong side row.

Shape front opening

Cast off 3 sts at beg of next 2 rows. 112 (118:126) sts.

Cont straight until work measures 30 (33:36) cm/11¾ (13:14) in from beg of rib, ending with a wrong side row.

Divide for armholes

Next row K26 (28:30) sts and turn; leaving rem sts on a spare needle.

Working on these 26 (28:30) sts only for Right Front, cont in garter st for a further 9 (10:11) cm/3½ (4:4¼) in, ending with a wrong side row.

Shape neck

Cast off 3 sts at beg of next row. Dec one st at neck edge on every row until 19 (20:21) sts rem. Cont straight until work measures 44 (48:52) cm/17¼ (19:20½) in from beg of rib, ending with a right side row.

Shape shoulder

Cast off 10 (10:11) sts at beg of next row. K 1 row. Cast off rem 9 (10:10) sts.

With right side facing, rejoin yarn to rem sts and K60 (62:66) sts, turn, leaving rem sts on a spare needle. Working on these sts only for Back, cont in garter st until work measures same as Right Front to shoulder shaping, ending with a wrong side row.

Shape shoulders

Cast off 10 (10:11) sts at beg of next 2 rows and 9 (10:10) sts at beg of foll 2 rows. Leave rem 22 (22:24) sts on a holder.

With right side facing, rejoin yarn to rem sts for Left Front and K to end.

Complete to match Right Front, reversing shapings.

Left Mitten

***With 4 mm (No 8/US 5) needles and A, cast on 16 sts. K 1 row.

Next row K1, M1, K6, M1, K2, M1, K6, M1, K1. K 1 row.

Next row K1, M1, K8, M1, K2, M1, K8, M1, K1. K 1 row.

Next row K1, M1, K10, M1, K2, M1, K10, M1, K1.

2nd and 3rd sizes only

K 1 row.

Next row K1, M1, K12, M1, K2, M1, K12, M1, K1.

All sizes

K 3 rows.

Next row K1, M1, K12 (16:14), [M1, K2] 1 (0:1) time, M1, K12 (15:14), [M1, K1] 1 (0:1) time. 32 (34:36) sts.

K 25 (29:33) rows. Change to M and K 1 row.***

Work Left Sleeve as follows:

Change to 3¼ mm (No 10/US 3) needles.

Next row P0 (1:0), [K1, P1] 8 (8:9) times, turn.

Work on this set of sts only.

Next row [K1, P1] to last 0 (1:0) st, K0 (1:0). Rib 1 row.

1st buttonhole row Rib 3, cast off 1, rib to last 4 sts, cast off 1, rib to end.

2nd buttonhole row Rib 3, cast on 1, rib to last 3 sts, cast on 1, rib to end.

Rib 2 rows. Cast off in rib.

With 3¼ mm (No 10/US 3) needles and wrong side facing, join M yarn to rem sts, cast on 8 (9:9) sts, P0 (1:1), [K1, P1] to last 0 (1:0) st, K0 (1:0).

Next row Cast on 8 (8:9) sts, P0 (1:1), [K1, P1] to last 0 (1:1) st, K0 (1:1). 32 (34:36) sts. Rib 4 rows.

****Next row Rib 3 (3:4), M1, [rib 5 (4:3),

M1] to last 4 (3:5) sts, rib to end. 38 (42:46) sts.

Change to 4 mm (No 8/US 5) needles and cont in garter st, inc one st at each end of every foll 3rd (4th:4th) row until there are 62 (66:70) sts. Cont straight until sleeve measures 14 (16:18) cm/5½ (6¼:7) in from beg of rib, ending with a wrong side row. Cast off loosely.

Right Mitten

Work as Left Mitten from *** to ***.

Work Right Sleeve as follows:

Change to 3¼ mm (No 10/US 3) needles.

Next row Cast on 8 (9:9) sts, K0 (0:1), [P1, K1] to last 0 (1:0) st, P0 (1:0).

Next row K0 (1:0), [P1, K1] 8 (8:9) times, turn.

Work on this set of sts only. Rib 1 row.

1st buttonhole row Rib 3, cast off 1, rib to last 4 sts, cast off 1, rib to end.

2nd buttonhole row Rib 3, cast on 1, rib to last 3 sts, cast on 1, rib to end.

Rib 2 rows. Cast off in rib.

With 3¼ mm (No 10/US 3) needles and right side facing, join M yarn to rem sts, cast on 8 (8:9) sts, K0 (0:1), [P1, K1] to last 0 (0:1) st, P0 (0:1). Rib 4 rows.

Complete as Left Sleeve from **** to end.

Neckband

Join shoulder seams.

With 3¼ mm (No 10/US 3) needles, M and right side facing, pick up and K 19 (20:21) sts up right front neck, K across 22 (22:24) sts on back neck holder, inc 1 st at centre, pick up and K 19 (20:21) sts down left front neck. 61 (63:67) sts.

1st row (wrong side) P1, [K1, P1] to end.

2nd row K1, [P1, K1] to end.

Rep last 2 rows twice more.

Next row Rib 5 and slip these sts onto a safety pin, rib 5 (5:4), inc in next st, [rib 9 (6:7), inc in next st] to last 10 (10:9) sts, rib 5 (5:4), slip last 5 sts onto a safety pin. 56 (60:64) sts.

Work Hood as follows:

Change to 4 mm (No 8/US 5) needles.

Cont in garter st until work measures 12 (14:16) cm/4¾ (5½:6¼) in from top of rib, ending with a wrong side row.

Shape top

Next row K37 (39:41) sts, K2 tog, turn.

Next row K19, K2 tog tbl, turn.

Next row K19, K2 tog, turn.

Rep last 2 rows until all sts are decreased on either side of hood. Leave rem 20 sts on a holder.

Hood Edging

With 3¼ mm (No 10/US 3) needles, right side facing and M, rib 5 sts from right side of hood safety pin, pick up and K 26 (29:32) sts up right side of hood, K across sts on holder, dec one st, pick up and K 26 (29:32) sts down left side of hood, rib 5 sts on left side safety pin. 81 (87:93) sts.

Rib 7 rows. Cast off in rib.

Buttonhole Band

With 3¼ mm (No 10/US 3) needles and M and right side facing, pick up and K 89 (99:109) sts evenly along right side edge of front opening to top of hood edging. Work 3

rows in rib as given for neckband.

1st buttonhole row Rib 3, [cast off 2, rib 13 (15:17) sts more] 5 times, cast off 2, rib to end.

2nd buttonhole row Rib to end, casting on 2 sts over those cast off in previous row. Rib 4 rows. Cast off in rib.

Button Band

Work to match Buttonhole Band, omitting buttonholes.

To Make Up

Join foot and leg seams, then back crotch seam. Join front crotch and centre seam to front opening. Overlap buttonhole band over button band and catch down to base of opening. Join side seam of mittens, leaving buttonhole band free. Join sleeve seams. Sew in sleeves. Sew on buttons to button band and cuffs.*****

Outer Ears (Make 2)

With 4 mm (No 8/US 5) needles and A, cast on 5 sts. Work in garter st, inc one st at each end of 2 foll alt rows. 9 sts. Cont straight until work measures 8 cm/3 in from beg. Cast off.

Inner Ears (Make 2)

With 3¼ mm (No 10/US 3) needles and Dark Grey, work as given for outer ears. Join paired pieces together. Fold cast off edges in half and sew through all thicknesses to each side of hood.

Tail

With 4 mm (No 8/US 5) needles and A, cast on 16 sts. Work in garter st for 7 cm/2¾ in. Cast off. Fold in half lengthwise and join seam. Attach to top of back crotch seam.

Bunny

Work as given for Lamb to *****, but using M only.

Outer Ears (Make 2)

With 4 mm (No 8/US 5) needles and M, cast on 5 sts. Work in garter st, inc one st at each end of every 3rd row until there are 13 sts. Cont straight for a further 7 cm/2¾ in. Dec one st at each end of next and every foll 3rd row until 5 sts rem. K 2 rows. Cast off.

Inner Ears (Make 2)

With 3¼ mm (No 10/US 3) needles and Pink, work as given for outer ears. Join paired pieces together. Fold cast off edges in half and sew through all thicknesses to each side of hood.

Tail

With White, make a pompon and attach to top of back crotch seam.

Chick Cardigan and Bootees

SEE PAGE
20

MATERIALS

Cardigan : 3 × 50g balls of Hayfield Raw Cotton Classics 4 ply in main colour (M). 1 × 50g ball of same in contrast colour (A). Small amounts of any 4 ply in 2 contrast colours (B and C). 7 buttons.

Bootees : 1 × 50g ball of Hayfield Raw Cotton Classics 4 ply in main colour (M). Small amounts of same in 2 contrast colours (A and B). 1 pair each of 2¾ mm (No 12/US 1) and 3¼ mm (No 10/US 3) knitting needles.

MEASUREMENTS

To fit age	0–3 months	
All round at chest	52 cm	20½ in
Length to shoulder	23 cm	9 in
Sleeve seam	14 cm	5½ in

TENSION

28 sts and 36 rows to 10 cm/4 in over st st on 3¼ mm (No 10/US 3) needles.

ABBREVIATIONS

See page 39.

NOTE

When working Fair Isle borders, strand yarn not in use loosely across wrong side. Use separate length of yarn for each motif and twist yarns together on wrong side when changing colour to avoid holes.

Cardigan

Main Part (work in one piece to armholes). With 2¾ mm (No 12/US 1) needles and B, cast on 141 sts. Change to M.

1st row (right side) K1, [P1, K1] to end. Change to A.

2nd row P1, [K1, P1] to end.

With A, cont in rib until work measures 3 cm/1¼ in from beg, ending with a wrong side row.

Change to 3¼ mm (No 10/US 3) needles and M.

Work border patt as follows:

Beg with a K row and working in st st throughout, work 2 rows.

3rd row 1C, [1M, 1C] to end.

4th row 1M, [1C, 1M] to end.

Work 4 rows in M.

9th row 1M, [1C, 1M, 1B, 1M] to end.

10th row 1B, [1M, 1B] to end.

11th row 1M, [1B, 1M, 1A, 1M] to end.

12th row As 10th row.

13th row As 9th row.

Now work patt from chart, reading K rows from right to left and P rows from left to right.

1st row Work across 1st row of chart as follows: 35 sts from W to X, then 71 sts from W to Z and 35 sts from Y to Z.

2nd row Work across 2nd row of chart as follows: 35 sts from Z to Y, then 71 sts from

Z to W and 35 sts from X to W.

These 2 rows set patt. Cont in patt as set, working appropriate rows of chart until work measures 13 cm/5 in from beg, ending with a wrong side row.

Divide for armholes

Next row Patt 35, turn. Work on these 35 sts only for Right Front.

Keeping patt correct, cont without shaping until work measures 20 cm/8 in from beg, ending with a wrong side row.

Shape neck

Cast off 5 sts at beg of next row. Dec one st at neck edge on every row until 24 sts rem.

Cont without shaping for a few rows until work measures 23 cm/9 in from beg, ending with a right side row.

Shape shoulder

Cast off 12 sts at beg of next row. Work 1 row. Cast off rem 12 sts.

With right side facing, rejoin yarn to rem sts and patt 71 sts, turn. Work on these 71 sts only for Back. Cont without shaping until Back measures same as Right Front to shoulder shaping, ending with a wrong side row.

Shape shoulders

Cast off 12 sts at beg of next 4 rows. Leave rem 23 sts on a holder.

With right side facing, rejoin yarn to rem 35 sts for Left Front and patt to end. Complete to match Right Front, reversing all shaping.

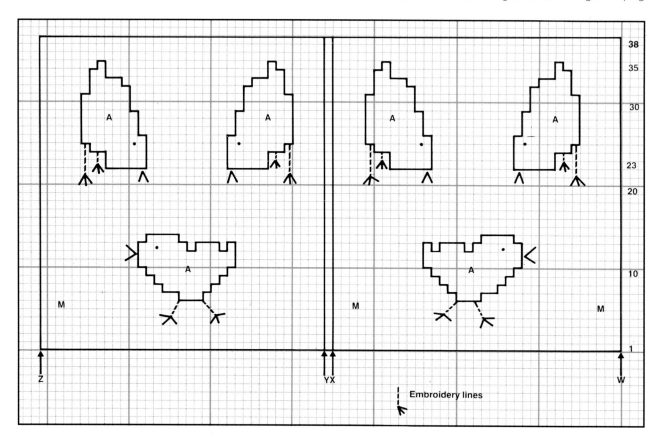

Embroidery lines

Sleeves

With 2¾ mm (No 12/US 1) needles and B, cast on 37 sts.
Change to M and work in rib as given for Back for 1 row. Change to A and cont in rib until work measures 3 cm/1¼ in from beg, ending with a wrong side row and inc 8 sts evenly across last row. 45 sts.
Change to 3¼ mm (No 10/US 3) needles. Work border patt as given for Back, *at the same time,* inc one st at each end of every foll 3rd row. Work 7 rows in M only, inc one st at each end of 2nd and foll 3rd row. 57 sts.
Now work patt from chart as follows:
1st row With M, K twice in first st, K10, work across 35 sts of 23rd row of chart from W to X, with M, K10, K twice in last st.
2nd row P12 M, work across 35 sts of 24th row of chart from X to W, P12 M.
These 2 rows set patt. Cont in patt as set until 35th row of chart has been worked, *at the same time,* inc one st at each end of 2nd and foll 3rd row, working inc sts in M. 63 sts.
Cont without shaping and M only for a few rows until work measures 14 cm/5½ in from beg, ending with a wrong side row. Cast off.

Neckband

Join shoulder seams. With 2¾ mm (No 12/US 1) needles, M and right side facing, pick up and K 20 sts up right front neck, K across 23 sts on back neck, pick up and K 20 sts down left front neck. 63 sts. Change to A and work 9 rows in rib as given for Back. Change to M and rib 1 row. Change to B and cast off in rib.

Buttonhole Band

With 2¾ mm (No 12/US 1) needles, M and right side facing, pick up and K 63 sts evenly along front edge of Right Front. Change to A, work 4 rows in rib as given for Back.
1st buttonhole row Rib 3, [cast off 2, rib 6 sts more] 6 times, cast off 2, rib to end.
2nd buttonhole row Rib to end, casting on 2 sts over those cast off in previous row. Rib 3 rows. Change to M and rib 1 row. Change to B and cast off in rib.

Button Band

Work to match Buttonhole Band, omitting buttonholes.

To Make Up

Sew on sleeves, placing centre of sleeves to shoulder seams. Join sleeve seams. Sew on buttons. With B and straight stitch (see diagram page 70), embroider legs, feet, eyes and beaks on chicks.

Bootees

With M only, work as Bootees of Striped Sweater with Zig Zag Collar (see page 44) until the strap has been completed. Using B, complete to match Bootees of Striped Sweater with Zig Zag Collar, omitting edging. With A, make 2 pompons and attach one to each Bootee.

Classic Jacket

SEE PAGE 21

MATERIALS

4 (5:6) 50g balls of Hayfield Pure Wool Classics DK.
1 pair of 4 mm (No 8/US 5) knitting needles.
Medium size crochet hook.
8 buttons.

MEASUREMENTS

To fit age
6–12 (12–24:24–36) months
All round at chest
59 (64:69) cm   23¼ (25¼:27¼) in
Length to shoulder
26 (30:34) cm   10¼ (11¾:13½) in
Sleeve seam
16 (20:24) cm   6¼ (8:9½) in

TENSION

23 sts and 38 rows to 10 cm/4 in over moss st on 4 mm (No 8/US 5) needles.

ABBREVIATIONS

See page 39.

Back

With 4 mm (No 8/US 5) needles, cast on 67 (73:79) sts.
1st row K1, [P1, K1] to end.
This row forms moss st patt. Cont in moss st until work measures 26 (30:34) cm/10¼ (11¾:13½) in from beg.
Shape shoulders
Cast off 10 (11:12) sts at beg of next 4 rows. Cast off rem 27 (29:31) sts.

Pocket Flaps (Make 4)

With 4 mm (No 8/US 5) needles, cast on 17 sts.
Work 10 rows in moss st patt as given for Back. Leave these sts on a holder.

Left Front

With 4 mm (No 8/US 5) needles, cast on 37 (41:43) sts.
Cont in moss st patt as given for Back until work measures 8 (9:10) cm/3 (3½:4) in from beg, ending at side edge.
**Place pocket flap
Next row (right side) Moss st 8 (10:10) sts, now place one pocket flap sts in front of work, then taking one st from each needle and working them together, moss st across these 17 sts, moss st to end.**
Cont in moss st until work measures 20 (23:26) cm/8 (9:10¼) in from beg, ending with a wrong side row.
Rep from ** to ** once more.
Cont in moss st until work measures 22 (26:30) cm/8¾ (10¼:11¾) in from beg, ending at front edge.
Shape neck
Cast off 7 (9:9) sts at beg of next row. Keeping moss st correct, dec one st at neck edge on every row until 20 (22:24) sts rem. Cont without shaping until work measures same as Back to shoulder shaping, ending at side edge.
Shape shoulder
Cast off 10 (11:12) sts at beg of next row.

Moss st 1 row. Cast off rem 10 (11:12) sts.
Mark front edge with pins indicating buttons, first one to come 7 (8:9) cm/2¾ (3:3½) in up from cast on edge and last one 1 cm/¼ in down from neck edge and rem 2 spaced evenly between.

Right Front

With 4 mm (No 8/US 5) needles, cast on 37 (41:43) sts.
Cont in moss st patt as given for Back until work measures 7 (8:9) cm/2¾ (3:3½) in from beg, ending at front edge.
1st buttonhole row (right side) Moss st 2, cast off 3, moss st to end.
2nd buttonhole row Moss st to end, casting on 3 sts over those cast off in previous row. Moss st 2 rows.
***Place pocket flap
Next row Moss st 12 (14:16), now place one pocket flap sts in front of work, then taking one st from each needle and working them together, moss st across these 17 sts, moss st to end.***
Complete to match Left Front, making 3 more buttonholes at pin positions as before and placing 2nd flap as given from *** to ***.

Sleeves

With 4 mm (No 8/US 5) needles, cast on 37 (39:41) sts.
Work in moss st patt as given for Back, *at the same time,* inc one st at each end of every foll 5th (6th:7th) row until there are 53 (57:61) sts.
Cont without shaping until work measures 16 (20:24) cm/6¼ (8:9½) in from beg. Cast off.

To Make Up

Join shoulder seams. Sew on sleeves, placing centre of sleeves to shoulder seams. Join side and sleeve seams.
Crochet edging
With crochet hook and right side facing, work 1 row of double crochet along cast on edge of Back, Right Front, up Right Front, around neck, down Left Front, then along cast on edge of Left Front. DO NOT TURN. Now work 1 row of backward double crochet (double crochet worked from left to right-corded st). Fasten off.
Work crochet edging along cast on edge of Sleeves and round 3 free edges of each Pocket Flap.
Sew on 4 buttons to front edge of Left Front and one to centre of each Flap.

Peasant Style Cardigan

SEE PAGE
22

MATERIALS
4 (4:5) 50g balls of Hayfield Pure Wool Classics DK in main (A).
1 ball of same in 4 colours (B, C, D and E).
1 pair each of 3¼ mm (No 10/US 3) and 4 mm (No 8/US 5) knitting needles.
5 buttons.

MEASUREMENTS
To fit age
        1 (2:3) years
All round at chest
      64 (69:74) cm   25¼ (27:29) in
Length to shoulder
      30 (33:37) cm   11¾ (13:14½) in
Sleeve seam
      23 (26:29) cm   9 (10¼:11½) in

TENSION
22 sts and 28 rows to 10 cm/4 in over st st using 4 mm (No 8/US 5) needles.

ABBREVIATIONS
See page 39.

NOTE
When working motifs, use a separate length of yarn for each section and twist yarns together on wrong side when changing colour to avoid holes.
When working Fair Isle bands, strand yarn not in use loosely across wrong side to keep fabric elastic.

TO MAKE

Back
With 3¼ mm (No 10/US 3) needles and A, cast on 71 (77:83) sts.
1st row (right side) K1, [P1, K1] to end.
2nd row P1, [K1, P1] to end.
Rep these 2 rows until work measures 3 cm/1¼ in from beg, ending with a wrong side row and inc 6 sts evenly across last row. 77 (83:89) sts.
Change to 4 mm (No 8/US 5) needles.
Beg with a K row and working in st st throughout, cont in patt from chart as indicated for Back, reading K rows from right to left and P rows from left to right, until 76 (84:94) rows of patt in all have been worked.
Shape shoulders
Keeping patt correct, cast off 12 (13:14) sts at beg of next 4 rows. Leave rem 29 (31:33) sts on a holder.

Left Front
With 3¼ mm (No 10/US 3) needles and A, cast on 33 (35:39) sts.
Work in rib as given for Back for 3 cm/1¼ in, ending with a wrong side row and inc 3 (4:3) sts evenly across last row. 36 (39:42) sts.
Change to 4 mm (No 8/US 5) needles.
Beg with a K row and working in st st throughout, cont in patt from chart as indicated for Left Front until 65 (69:79) rows of patt in all have been worked.
Shape neck
Keeping patt correct, cast off 4 (5:6) sts at beg of next row. Dec one st at neck edge on every row until 24 (26:28) sts rem.
Cont without shaping until work measures same as Back to shoulder shaping, ending with a wrong side row.
Shape shoulders
Cast off 12 (13:14) sts at beg of next row. Patt 1 row. Cast off rem 12 (13:14) sts.

Right Front
Work as given for Left Front, reversing all shaping and working patt from chart as indicated for Right Front.

Sleeves
With 3¼ mm (No 10/US 3) needles and A, cast on 37 (39:41) sts.
Work in rib as given for Back for 3 cm/1¼ in, ending with a wrong side row and inc 6 sts evenly across last row. 43 (45:47) sts.
Change to 4 mm (No 8/US 5) needles.
Beg with a K row and working in st st throughout, cont in patt from chart as indicated for Sleeve, *at the same time,* inc one st at each end of 5th row, then foll 16th row, foll 10th row and foll 9th row, then on every foll 5th row until there are 55 (59:63) sts.
Cont without shaping until 56 (64:72) rows of patt in all have been worked. Cast off.

Neckband
Join shoulder seams.
With 3¼ mm (No 10/US 3) needles, right side facing and A, pick up and K 17 (19:19) sts up right front neck, K across 29 (31:33) sts on back neck, pick up and K 17 (19:19) sts down left front neck. 63 (69:71) sts.
Work 9 rows in rib as given for Back. Cast off in rib.

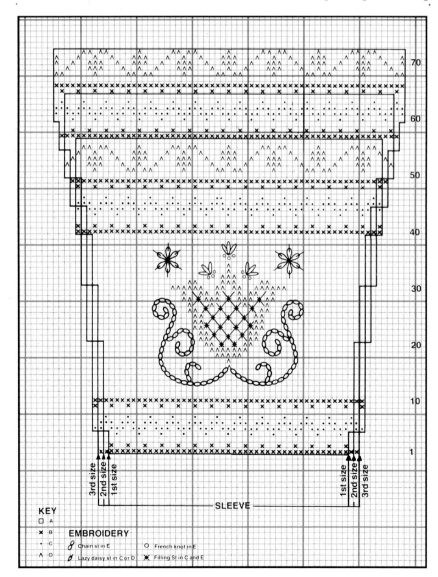

70

60

50

40

30

20

10

1

3rd size 2nd size 1st size

1st size 2nd size 3rd size

SLEEVE

KEY
☐ A
✕ B
• C
∧ D

EMBROIDERY
ℰ Chain st in E
ℰ Lazy daisy st in C or D
○ French knot in E
✗ Filling St in C and E

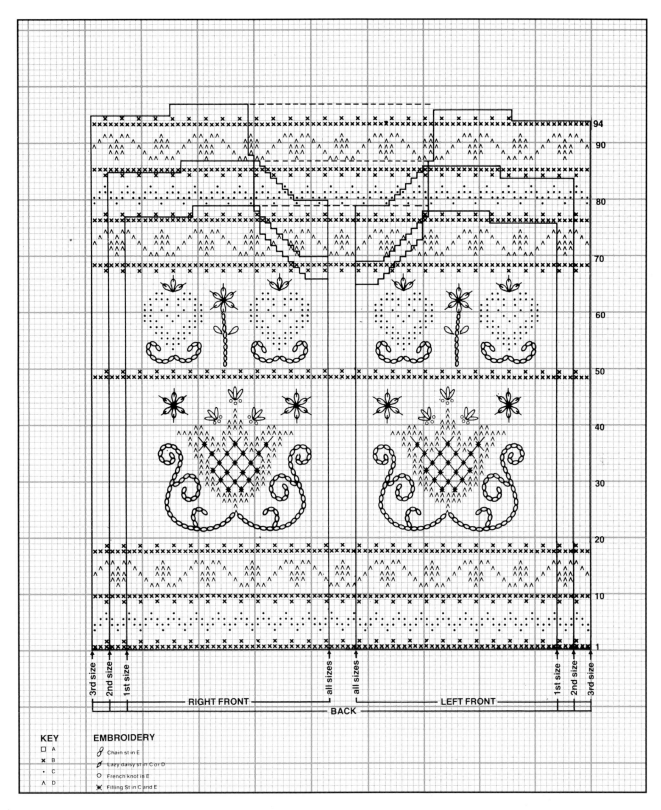

KEY

□	A
×	B
·	C
∧	D

EMBROIDERY

ℰ	Chain st in E
ℓ	Lazy daisy st in C or D
O	French knot in E
✕	Filling St in C and E

Buttonhole Band

With 3¼ mm (No 10/US 3) needles, right side facing and A, pick up and K 73 (81:89) sts evenly along straight edge of Right Front to top of neckband.
Beg with a 2nd row, work 3 rows in rib as given for Back.

Buttonhole row Rib 3, [P2 tog, yrn, rib 14 (16:18) sts] 4 times, P2 tog, yrn, rib to end. Rib 4 rows. Cast off in rib.

Button Band

Work to match Buttonhole Band, omitting buttonholes.

To Make Up

Work embroidery in colours and stitches as indicated on chart. (See pages 61, 70 & 75 for diagrams.)
Sew on sleeves, placing centre of sleeves to shoulder seams. Join side and sleeve seams. Sew on buttons.

Navajo Jacket

MATERIALS
4 × 50g balls of Hayfield Pure Wool Classics DK in main colour (M).
2 balls of same in each of 2 colours (A and B).
1 ball of same in each of 3 colours (C, D and E).
1 pair each of 3¼ mm (No 10/US 3) and 4 mm (No 8/US 5) knitting needles.
3 buttons.

MEASUREMENTS
To fit age
2 (3) years
All round at chest
74 (80) cm   29 (31½) in
Length to shoulder
37 (40) cm   14½ (15¾) in
Sleeve seam
25 (28) cm   10 (11) in

TENSION
23 sts and 24 rows to 10 cm/4 in over patt using 4 mm (No 8/US 5) needles.

ABBREVIATIONS
See page 39.

NOTE
When working in pattern, strand yarn not in use loosely across wrong side to keep fabric elastic.

Back
With 3¼ mm (No 10/US 3) needles and M, cast on 85 (93) sts. Beg with a K row, work 7 rows in st st.
Next row K to end for hem line.
Change to 4 mm (No 8/US 5) needles.
Beg with a K row and working in st st throughout, cont in patt from chart as indicated for Back, reading K rows from right to left and P rows from left to right, until work measures 35 (38) cm/13¾ (15) in from hem line, ending with a wrong side row.
Shape neck
Next row Patt 34 (36), cast off next 17 (21) sts, patt to end. Cont on last set of sts only. Patt 1 row. Cast off 3 sts at beg of next row and foll alt row. Cast off rem 28 (30) sts.
With wrong side facing, rejoin yarn to rem sts, cast off 3 sts, patt to end. Patt 1 row. Cast off 3 sts at beg of next row. Cast off rem 28 (30) sts.

Right Front
With 3¼ mm (No 10/US 3) needles and M, cast on 47 (51) sts. Beg with a K row, work 7 rows in st st.
Next row K to end for hem line.
Change to 4 mm (No 8/US 5) needles.
Beg with a K row and working in st st throughout, cont in patt from chart as indicated for Right Front until work measures 10 cm/4 in from hem line, ending with a wrong side row.
1st buttonhole row Patt 3, cast off 2, patt to end.

2nd buttonhole row Patt to last 3 sts, cast on 2, patt 3.
Patt 8 rows.
Rep last 10 rows once more then work the 2 buttonhole rows again.
Cont in patt for a few rows until work measures 19 (20) cm/7½ (8) in from hem line, ending with a wrong side row.
Shape neck
Keeping patt correct, cast off 5 sts at beg of next row.
Dec one st at neck edge on 9 foll right side rows then on every 3rd row until 28 (30) sts rem.
Cont without shaping until work measures same as Back to cast off edge, ending at side edge. Cast off.

Left Front
Following chart as indicated for Left Front, work as given for Right Front, omitting buttonholes and reversing neck shaping.

Sleeves
With 3¼ mm (No 10/US 3) needles and M, cast on 38 (42) sts. Work 5 cm/2 in in K1, P1 rib inc 7 (3) sts evenly along last row. 45 sts.
Change to 4 mm (No 8/US 5) needles.
Work in patt as given for 2nd size on Back, *at the same time* inc one st at each end of 5th row, then on every foll 3rd row until there are 71 (75) sts, working inc sts into patt.
Cont without shaping for a few rows until work measures 25 (28) cm/10 (11) in from beg, ending with a wrong side row. Cast off.

Collar
Join shoulder seams.
With 4 mm (No 8/US 5) needles and B, cast on 13 (15) sts.
Beg with a P row, work 7 (5) rows in st st inc one st at each end of every K row. 19 sts.
Next row (right side) With B, K twice in first st, K 1M, [3B, 1M] to last st, with B, K twice in last st.
Next row P 1B, [3M, 1B] to end.
With M, work 3 rows in st st inc one st at each end of every K row. 25 sts.
Beg with 60th row, cont in st st and patt from chart as indicated for Collar, *at the same time*, inc one st at each end of every alt row until there are 55 (61) sts, working inc sts into patt.
Patt 1 (5) rows straight.
Shape collar
Cont in M as follows:
1st row K to last 6 (7) sts, yf, sl 1, yb, turn.
2nd row Sl 1, P to last 6 (7) sts, yb, sl 1, yf, turn.
3rd row Sl 1, K to last 12 (14) sts, yf, sl 1, yb, turn.
4th row Sl 1, P to last 12 (14) sts, yb, sl 1, yf, turn.
5th row Sl 1, K to last 18 (21) sts, yf, sl 1, yb, turn.
6th row Sl 1, P to last 18 (21) sts, yb, sl 1, yf,

turn.
7th row Sl 1, K to last 24 (28) sts, yf, sl 1, yb, turn.
8th row Sl 1, P to last 24 (28) sts, yb, sl 1, yf, turn.
Work 2 rows across all sts.
Next 2 rows As 7th and 8th rows.
Next 2 rows As 5th and 6th rows.
Next 2 rows As 3rd and 4th rows.
Next 2 rows As 1st and 2nd rows.
Cont without shaping until this half of collar fits up right front neck to centre back neck. Work the other half of collar to match first half, but working decreases instead of increases. Cast off 13 (15) sts.

Right Front Facing
With 3¼ mm (No 10/US 3) needles and M, cast on 7 sts. Beg with a K row, cont in st st until work measures 7 cm/2¾ in, ending with a P row.
1st buttonhole row K3, cast off 2, K to end.
2nd buttonhole row P2, cast on 2, P3.
Work 8 rows.
Rep last 10 rows once more then work the 2 buttonhole rows again. Work 2 (4) rows.
Cast off.

Left Front Facing
Work as Right Front Facing, omitting buttonholes.

To Make Up
Sew on sleeves, placing centre of sleeves to shoulder seams. Join side and sleeve seams. Turn hem to wrong side and slip stitch in position. Close opening at front edges.
Beg at top of hem, join facings to front edges, matching buttonholes.
With right sides together, sew one long edge of collar in place, matching patterns and sewing cast on/cast off sts of collar to top of facings and sts cast off at neck edge. Turn collar and facings to wrong side and slip stitch in position. Catch down facings to hem. Neaten buttonholes. Sew on buttons.

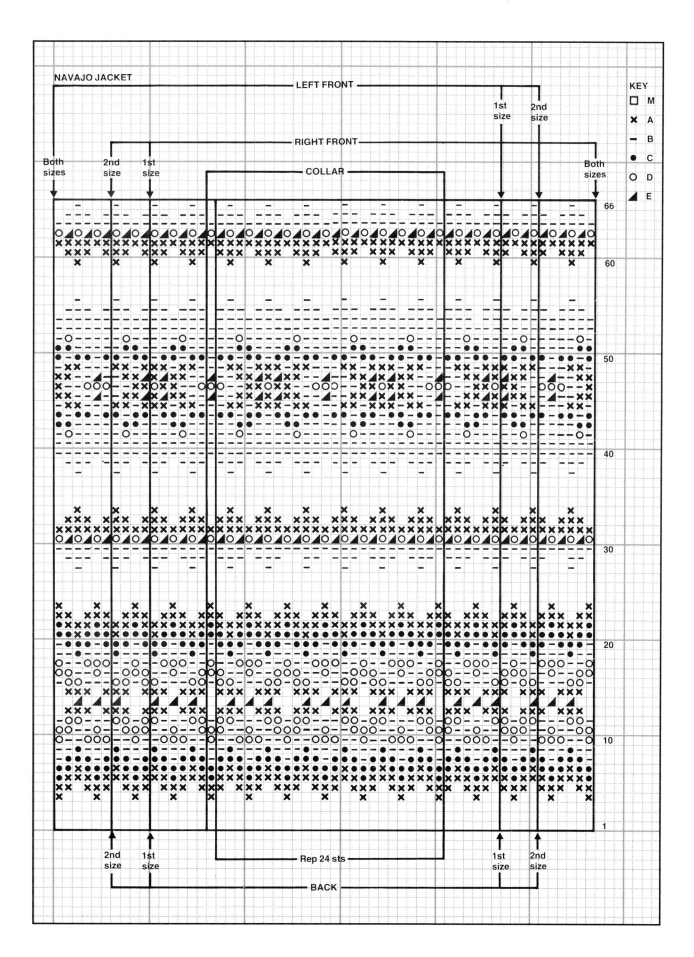

Folkloric Cardigan

SEE PAGE
24

MATERIALS

3 (4) 50g balls of Hayfield Pure Wool Classics DK or 3 × 50g balls of Hayfield Grampian DK in main colour (M).
1 ball of same in each of 4 colours (A, B, C and D).
1 pair each of 3¼ mm (No 10/US 3) and 4 mm (No 8/US 5) knitting needles.
Medium size crochet hook.

MEASUREMENTS

To fit age
6–12 (12–18) months
All round at chest
64 (72) cm   25¼ (28¼) in
Length to shoulder
26 (31) cm   10¼ (12¼) in
Sleeve seam
17 (20) cm   6¾ (8) in

TENSION

22 sts and 28 rows to 10 cm/4 in over st st using 4 mm (No 8/US 5) needles.

ABBREVIATIONS

See page 39.

NOTE

When working border pattern, strand yarn not in use loosely across wrong side to keep fabric elastic.
When working motifs, use a separate length of yarn for each section and twist yarns together on wrong side when changing colour to avoid holes.
If preferred, the front edge border pattern or small areas of contrast on motifs may be Swiss Darned when knitting is complete.

Back

With 4 mm (No 8/US 5) needles and M, cast on 71 (79) sts.
1st row K1, [P1, K1] to end.
This row forms moss st.
Rep this row 3 times more.
Beg with a K row, work 2 rows in st st.
Work lower border patt as follows:
**1st row (right side) K3M, [1A, 3M] to end.
2nd row P1A, [1M, 1A] to end.
3rd row K1M, [1A, 1M, 1B, 1M] to last 2 sts, 1A, 1M.
4th row As 2nd row.
5th row As 1st row.**
Beg with a P row, work 4 rows in st st and M only.
Now work motifs from chart 1 and chart 2 as follows:
1st row (wrong side) P10 (12) M, P across 15 sts from X to Y (thus reversing motif) of row 1 of chart 1, P3 (5) M, P across 15 sts from Y to X of row 1 of chart 2, P3 (5) M, P across 15 sts from Y to X of row 1 of chart 1, P10 (12) M.
2nd row K10 (12) M, K across 15 sts from X to Y of row 2 of chart 1, K3 (5) M, K across 15 sts from X to Y of row 2 of chart 2, K3 (5) M, K across 15 sts from Y to X of row 2 of chart 1, K10 (12) M.
3rd to 10th rows Rep 1st and 2nd rows 4

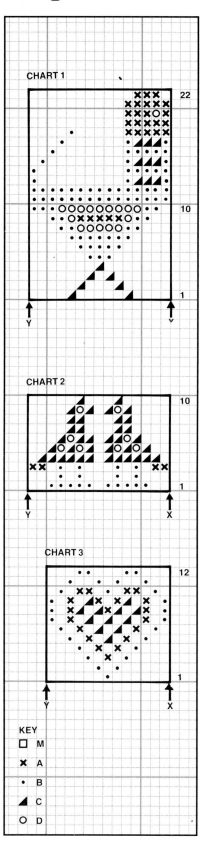

CHART 1

22

10

1

Y

CHART 2

10

1

Y   X

CHART 3

12

1

Y   X

KEY
☐ M
✖ A
• B
◢ C
○ D

times more, but working 3rd to 10th rows of chart 1 and chart 2.
11th row P10 (12) M, P across 15 sts from X to Y of row 11 of chart 1, P21 (25) M, P across 15 sts from Y to X of row 11 of chart 1, P10 (12) M.
12th row K10 (12) M, K across 15 sts from X to Y of row 12 of chart 1, K21 (25) M, K across 15 sts from Y to X of row 12 of chart 1, K10 (12) M.
13th to 22nd rows Rep 11th and 12th rows 5 times more, but working 13th to 22nd rows of chart 1.
Beg with a P row, cont in st st and M only until work measures 26 (31) cm/10¼ (12¼) in from beg, ending with a P row.
Shape shoulders
Cast off 11 (12) sts at beg of next 4 rows.
Leave rem 27 (31) sts on a holder.

Left Front

With 4 mm (No 8/US 5) needles and M, cast on 35 (39) sts.
Work 4 rows in moss st as given for Back.
Next row K to last 4 sts, moss st 4.
Next row Moss st 4, P to end.
Work lower border patt as follows:
1st row (right side) K1A, [3M, 1A] to last 6 sts, with M, K2, moss st 4.
2nd row With M, moss st 4, P1M, [1A, 1M] to end.
3rd row K1B, 1M, 1A, [1M, 1B, 1M, 1A] to last 4 sts, with M, moss st 4.
4th row As 2nd row.
5th row As 1st row.
Work front edge border patt as follows:
1st row (wrong side) With M, moss st 4, [P1 M, 1A] twice, with M, P to end.
2nd row With M, K to last 9 sts, K1A, 1M, 1B, 1M, 1A, with M, moss st 4.
3rd row As 1st row.
4th row With M, K to last 7 sts, K1A, with M, K2, moss st 4.
These 4 rows form front edge border patt.
Now work motif from chart 1 as follows:
1st row (wrong side) Border patt 9, P6 M, P across 15 sts from X to Y (thus reversing motif) of row 1 of chart 1, P5 (9) M.
2nd row K5 (9) M, K across 15 sts from Y to X of row 2 of chart 1, K6M, border patt 9.
3rd to 22nd rows Rep 1st and 2nd rows 10 times more, but working 3rd to 22nd rows of chart 1.
Next row Border patt 9, with M, P to end.
Next row With M, K to last 9 sts, border patt 9.
Rep last 2 rows until work measures approximately 16 (20) cm/6¼ (8) in from beg, ending with a 1st row of front edge border patt.
Work motif from chart 3 as follows:
1st row (right side) K6 (10) M, K across 13 sts from X to Y of row 1 of chart 3, K7M, border patt 9.
2nd row Border patt 9, P7M, P across 13 sts from Y to X of row 2 of chart 3, P6 (10) M.
3rd to 12th rows Rep 1st and 2nd rows 5 times more, but working 3rd to 12th rows of chart 3.

Next row With M, K to last 9 sts, border patt 9.
Next row Border patt 9, with M, P to end.
Work a further 1 (5) rows as set.
Keeping moss st at front edge, cont in M only, work 2 rows.

Shape neck
Cast off 5 (6) sts at beg of next row and 3 (4) sts at beg of foll alt row. Dec one st at neck edge on next 5 rows. 22 (24) sts.
Cont without shaping for a few rows until work measures same as Back to shoulder shaping, ending at side edge.

Shape shoulders
Cast off 11 (12) sts at beg of next row. Work 1 row. Cast off rem 11 (12) sts.

Right Front

With 4 mm (No 8/US 5) needles and M, cast on 35 (39) sts.
Work 4 rows in moss st as given for Back.
Next row Moss st 4, K to end.
Next row P to last 4 sts, moss st 4.
Work lower border patt as follows:
1st row (right side) With M, moss st 4, K2, [1A, 3M] to last st, 1A.
2nd row P1M, [1A, 1M] to last 4 sts, with M, moss st 4.
3rd row With M, moss st 4, K1A, [1M, 1B, 1M, 1A] to last 2 sts, 1M, 1B.
4th row As 2nd row.
5th row As 1st row.
Work front edge border patt as follows:
1st row (wrong side) With M, P to last 8 sts, [P1A, 1M] twice, with M, moss st 4.
2nd row With M, moss st 4, K1A, 1M, 1B, 1M, 1A, with M, K to end.
3rd row As 1st row.
4th row With M, moss st 4, K2M, 1A, with M, K to end.
These 4 rows form front edge border patt.
Now work motif from chart 1 as follows:
1st row (wrong side) P5 (9) M, P across 15 sts from Y to X of row 1 of chart 1, P6M, border patt 9.
2nd row Border patt 9, K6M, K across 15 sts from X to Y of row 2 of chart 1, K5 (9) M.
3rd to 22nd rows Rep 1st and 2nd rows 10 times more, but working 3rd to 22nd rows of chart 1.
Next row With M, P to last 9 sts, border patt 9.
Next row Border patt 9, with M, K to end.
Rep last 2 rows until work measures approximately 16 (20) cm/6¼ (8) in from beg, ending with a 1st row of front edge border patt.
Work motif from chart 3 as follows:
1st row (right side) Border patt 9, K7M, K across 13 sts from X to Y of row 1 of chart 3, K6 (10) M.
2nd row P6 (10) M, P across 13 sts from Y to X of row 2 of chart 3, P7M, border patt 9.
3rd to 12th rows Rep 1st and 2nd rows 5 times more, but working 3rd to 12th rows of chart 3.
Next row Border patt 9, with M, K to end.
Next row With M, P to last 9 sts, border patt 9.
Work a further 1 (5) rows as set. Keeping moss st at front edge, cont in M only, work 1 row.
Complete as Left Front.

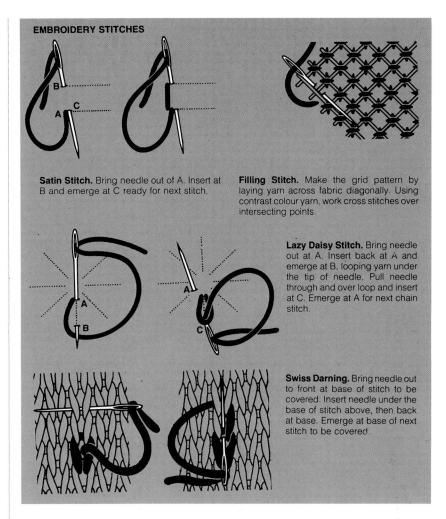

EMBROIDERY STITCHES

Satin Stitch. Bring needle out of A. Insert at B and emerge at C ready for next stitch.

Filling Stitch. Make the grid pattern by laying yarn across fabric diagonally. Using contrast colour yarn, work cross stitches over intersecting points.

Lazy Daisy Stitch. Bring needle out at A. Insert back at A and emerge at B, looping yarn under the tip of needle. Pull needle through and over loop and insert at C. Emerge at A for next chain stitch.

Swiss Darning. Bring needle out to front at base of stitch to be covered. Insert needle under the base of stitch above, then back at base. Emerge at base of next stitch to be covered.

Sleeves

With 3¼ mm (No 10/US 3) needles and M, cast on 37 (41) sts.
Work 4 rows in moss st as given for Back.
Change to 4 mm (No 8/US 5) needles.
Beg with a K row, work 2 rows in st st, inc one st at each end of last row. 39 (43) sts.
Work border patt as given for Back from ** to **
Beg with a P row, work 4 rows in st st and M only, inc one st at each end of first row. 41 (45) sts.
Now work motif from chart 2 as follows:
1st row (wrong side) P13 (15) M, P across 15 sts from Y to X of row 1 of chart 2, P13 (15) M.
2nd row K13 (15) M, K across 15 sts from X to Y of row 2 of chart 2, K13 (15) M.
3rd to 10th rows Rep 1st and 2nd rows 4 times more, but working 3rd to 10th rows of chart 2 and inc and work in M one st at each end of first and seventh rows. 45 (49) sts.
Beg P row, cont in st st and M only, *at the same time*, inc one st at each end of 5th and foll 6th row. 49 (53) sts.
Cont without shaping until work measures 17 (20) cm/6¾ (8) in from beg, ending with a P row. Cast off.

Neckband

Join shoulder seams.

With 3¼ mm (No 10/US 3) needles, right side facing and M, pick up and K 22 sts up right front neck, K across 27 (31) sts on back neck, pick up and K 22 sts down left front neck. 71 (75) sts.
Work 4 rows in moss st as given for Back.
Cast off in moss st.

To Make Up

Using B, work 5 lazy daisy stitches (see diagram above) on top of each head for cockscombe. Work 3 lazy daisy stitches in A at end of each tail, then fill centre of each stitch with satin stitch.
Embroider beak with C and crop in B.
Work Swiss Darning if necessary (see diagram above).
Sew on sleeves, placing centre of sleeves to shoulder seams. Join side and sleeve seams.

Crochet edging
With crochet hook, right side facing and B, work 1 row of double crochet along cast on edge of Back, Right Front, up Right Front, around neck and down Left Front, then along cast on edge of Left Front. DO NOT TURN. Now work 1 row of backwards double crochet (double crochet worked from left to right-corded st). Fasten off.
Work crochet edging in B along cast on edge of sleeves.

Hooded Fair Isle Jacket

SEE PAGE
25

MATERIALS

3 (4:4) 50g balls of Hayfield Pure Wool Classics DK in main colour (M).
3 balls of same in colour A.
2 (2:3) balls of same in colour B.
2 balls of same in colour C.
1 ball of same in 2 colours D and E.
1 pair each of 3¼ mm (No 10/US 3) and 4 mm (No 8/US 5) knitting needles.
6 buttons.

MEASUREMENTS

To fit age
    1 (2:3) years
All round at chest
    70 (75:80) cm   27½ (29½:31½) in
Length to shoulder
    34 (37:40) cm   13½ (14½:15¾) in
Sleeve seam
    21 (23:25) cm   8¼ (9:10) in

TENSION

23 sts and 24 rows to 10 cm/4 in over patt using 4 mm (No 8/US 5) needles.

ABBREVIATIONS

See page 39.

NOTE

When working in pattern, strand yarn not in use loosely across wrong side to keep fabric elastic.

Back

With 3¼ mm (No 10/US 3) needles and M, cast on 81 (87:93) sts.
Beg with a K row, work 7 rows in st st.
Next row K to end for hem line.
Change to 4 mm (No 8/US 5) needles.
Beg with a K row and working in st st throughout, cont in patt from chart as indicated for Back, reading K rows from right to left and P rows from left to right, until work measures 34 (37:40) cm/13½ (14½: 15¾) in from hem line, ending with a wrong side row. Cast off.

Right Front

With 3¼ mm (No 10/US 3) needles and M, cast on 55 (58:61) sts.
Beg with a K row, work 7 rows in st st.
Next row K to end for hem line.
Change to 4 mm (No 8/US 5) needles.
Beg with a K row and working in st st throughout, cont in patt from chart as indicated for Right Front until work measures 11.5 cm/4½ in from hem line, ending with a wrong side row.
1st buttonhole row Patt 3, cast off 3, patt to end.
2nd buttonhole row Patt to last 3 sts, cast on 3, patt 3.
Patt 10 (12:14) rows. Rep the 2 buttonhole rows again. Patt 2 rows.
Shape collar
Cast on 7 sts at beg of next row. Keeping patt correct, inc one st at front edge on next 10 rows then on every foll alt row until there are 84 (89:94) sts.

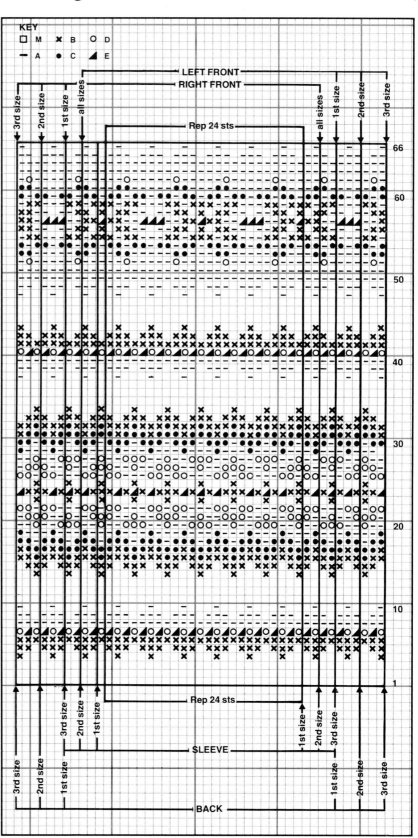

Cont without shaping until work measures same as Back to cast off edge, ending with a right side row.

Shape shoulder
Cast off 26 (28:30) sts at beg of next row. 58 (61:64) sts.

Shape right side hood
Cast on 15 (16:17) sts at beg of next 2 rows. 88 (93:98) sts.
Cont without shaping until hood measures 18 (20:23) cm/7 (8:9) in, ending with a wrong side row.

Shape top
Cast off 8 (9:9) sts at beg of next 8 rows.
Cast off rem 24 (21:26) sts.

Left Front

Following chart as indicated for Left Front, work as given for Right Front, reversing buttonhole rows and all shaping.

Sleeves

With 3¼ mm (No 10/US 3) needles and M, cast on 41 (45:49) sts.
1st row (right side) K1, [P1, K1] to end.
2nd row P1, [K1, P1] to end.
Rep these 2 rows until work measures 4 cm/1½ in from beg, ending with a wrong side row and inc 8 sts evenly across last row. 49 (53:57) sts.
Change to 4 mm (No 8/US 5) needles.
Beg with a K row and working in st st throughout, cont in patt from chart as indicated for Sleeves, *at the same time*, inc one st at each end of 3rd (4th:4th) and 3 foll alt rows then on every 3rd row until there are 69 (73:79) sts, working inc sts into patt.
Cont without shaping until work measures 21 (23:25) cm/8¼ (9:10) in from beg, ending with a wrong side row. Cast off.

Front Facings (Make 2)

With 3¼ mm (No 10/US 3) needles and M, cast on 9 sts.
Work 8.5 cm/3½ in in st st, ending with a P row.
1st buttonhole row K 3, cast off 3, K to end.
2nd buttonhole row P 3, cast on 3, P to end.
Work 10 (12:14) rows, then rep the 2 buttonhole rows again. Work 2 rows. Cast off.

To Make Up

Join shoulder seams. Join back, top and inside back seam of hood. Fold hood in half to inside, folding shaped part of collar to wrong side of fronts. Join cast on edges of hood to back neck then slip stitch collar in position. Sew on sleeves, placing centre of sleeves to shoulder seams. Join side and sleeve seams.
Fold hem to wrong side and slip stitch in place, closing opening at front edges. Sew on facings, sewing cast on edges to top of hem and cast off edges to cast on sts for collar. Neaten buttonholes. Sew on 2 buttons to right side of Left Front and 2 to wrong side of Right Front to correspond with buttonholes, then sew 2 buttons to right side of Right Front in same place as buttons on wrong side.

Tyrolean Cardigan

SEE PAGE 26

MATERIALS

4 (5:5) 50g balls of Hayfield Pure Wool Classics 4 ply in main colour (M).
Oddments of DK yarn in 3 colours for embroidery.
Pair each of 2¾ mm (No 12 /US 1) and 3¼ mm (No 10/US 3) knitting needles.
5 buttons.

MEASUREMENTS

To fit age
1 (2:3) years
All round at chest
66 (72:76) cm   26 (28¼:30) in
Length to shoulder
31 (34:37) cm   12¼ (13¼:14½) in
Sleeve seam
19 (22:25) cm   7½ (8¾:10) in

TENSION

28 sts and 36 rows to 10 cm/4 in over st st on 3¼ mm (No 10/US 3) needles.

ABBREVIATIONS

T2F = K into front of second st, then K first st, slipping both sts off needle together.
T2B = K into back of second st, then K first st, slipping both sts off needle together.
MB = [K1, P1, K1, P1, K1] all in next st, turn, K5, turn, P5, turn, K2 tog, K1, K2 tog, turn, P3 tog.
Also see page 39.

Panel A – worked over 4 sts.
1st row (right side) T2F, T2B.
2nd row P4.
3rd row T2B, T2F.
4th row As 2nd row.
These 4 rows form patt.

Panel B – worked over 19 sts.
1st row (right side) P6, T2B, K1, MB, K1, T2F, P6.
2nd row K6, P7, K6.
3rd row P5, T2B, K5, T2F, P5.
4th row K5, P9, K5.
5th row P4, T2B, K1, MB, K3, MB, K1, T2F, P4.
6th row K4, P11, K4.
7th row P3, T2B, K9, T2F, P3.
8th row K3, P13, K3.
9th row P2, T2B, K1, MB, K7, MB, K1, T2F, P2.
10th row K2, P15, K2.
11th row P1, T2B, K13, T2F, P1.
12th row K1, P17, K1.
13th row P1, K2, MB, K11, MB, K2, P1.
14th row As 12th row.
15th row P1, K17, P1.
16th row As 12th row.
These 16 rows form patt.

Back

With 2¾ mm (No 12/US 1) needles and M, cast on 86 (94:102) sts.
1st row (right side) K2, [P2, K2] to end.
2nd row P2, [K2, P2] to end.

Rep these 2 rows until work measures 4 cm/1½ in from beg, ending with a right side row.
Next row Rib 8 (4:5), [inc in next st, rib 3 (4:5) sts] to last 6 (0:1) sts, rib 6 (0:1). 104 (112:118) sts.
Change to 3¼ mm (No 10/US 3) needles.
Work in patt as follows:
1st row (right side) P4 (8:11), work 1st row of Panel A, [work 1st row of Panel B, then Panel A] 4 times, P4 (8:11).
2nd row K4 (8:11), work 2nd row of Panel A, [work 2nd row of Panel B, then Panel A] 4 times, K4 (8:11).
These 2 rows set patt. Cont in patt as set, working appropriate rows of Panels until work measures 18 (20:22) cm/7 (8:8¾) in from beg, ending with a wrong side row.

Shape armholes
Cast off 4 (5:5) sts at beg of next 2 rows.
Keeping patt correct, dec one st at each end of every row until 88 (92:96) sts rem.
Cont without shaping until work measures 31 (34:37) cm/12¼ (13¼:14½) in from beg, ending with a wrong side row.

Shape shoulders
Cast off 9 (10:10) sts at beg of next 4 rows and 9 (9:10) sts at beg of foll 2 rows. Leave rem 34 (34:36) sts on a holder.

Left Front

With 2¾ mm (No 12/US 1) needles and M, cast on 42 (46:50) sts. Work in rib as given for Back for 4 cm/1½ in, ending with a right side row.
Next row Rib 3 (5:6), inc in next st, [rib 4 (4:5), inc in next st] to last 3 (5:7) sts, rib to end. 50 (54:57) sts.
Change to 3¼ mm (No 10/US 3) needles.
Work in patt as follows:
1st row (right side) P4 (8:11), [work 1st row of Panel A, then Panel B] twice.
2nd row [Work 2nd row of Panel B, then Panel A] twice, K4 (8:11).
These 2 rows set patt. Cont in patt as set, working appropriate rows of Panels until work measures same as Back to armhole shaping, ending with a wrong side row.

Shape armhole
Cast off 4 (5:5) sts at beg of next row. Dec one st at armhole edge on every row until 42 (44:46) sts rem.
Cont without shaping until work measures 27 (30:33) cm/10¾ (11¾:13) in from beg, ending with a right side row.

Shape neck
Cast off 8 (8:9) sts at beg of next row. Dec one st at neck edge on next 7 rows. 27 (29:30) sts.
Cont without shaping until work measures same as Back to shoulder shaping, ending with a wrong side row.

Shape shoulder
Cast off 9 (10:10) sts at beg of next row and foll alt row. Work 1 row. Cast off rem 9 (9:10) sts.

continued overleaf

Right Front

Work as given for Left Front, reversing all shaping and patt as follows:

1st row (right side) [Work 1st row of Panel B, then Panel A] twice, P4 (8:11).

2nd row K4 (8:11), [work 2nd row of Panel A, then Panel B] twice.

Sleeves

With 2¾ mm (No 12/US 1) needles and M, cast on 38 (42:42) sts. Work in rib as given for Back for 4 cm/1½ in, ending with a right side row.

Next row Rib 2 (4:4), [inc in next st, rib 1 (2:1), inc in next st, rib 2] to last 1 (2:3) sts, rib to end. 52 (54:56) sts.

Change to 3¼ mm (No 10/US 3) needles. Work in patt as follows:

1st row (right side) P1 (2:3), work 1st row of Panel A, [work 1st row of Panel B, then Panel A] twice, P1 (2:3).

2nd row K1 (2:3), work 2nd row of Panel A, [work 2nd row of Panel B, then Panel A] twice, K1 (2:3).

These 2 rows set patt. Cont in patt as set, working appropriate rows of Panels, *at the same time*, inc one st at each end of next and every foll 4th row until there are 72 (80:86) sts, working inc sts into reverse st st.

Cont without shaping until work measures 19 (22:25) cm/7½ (8¾:10) in from beg, ending with a wrong side row.

Shape top

Cast off 4 (5:5) sts at beg of next 2 rows. Dec one st at each end of next 7 rows, then on every foll alt row until 28 (30:32) sts rem, ending with a wrong side row. Cast off.

Buttonhole Band

With 2¾ mm (No 12/US 1) needles, right side facing and M, pick up and K 78 (86:94) sts evenly along front edge of Right Front. Work 3 rows in rib as given for Back.

1st buttonhole row Rib 3, [cast off 3, rib 15 (17:19) sts more] 3 times, cast off 3, rib to end.

2nd buttonhole row Rib to end, casting on 3 sts over those cast off in previous row. Rib 4 rows. Cast off in rib.

Button Band

Work to match Buttonhole Band, omitting buttonholes.

Neckband

Join shoulder seams.

With 2¾ mm (No 12/US 1) needles, M and right side facing, pick up and K 32 (32:33) sts across Buttonhole Band and right front neck, K across 34 (34:36) sts at back neck, pick up and K 32 (32:33) sts down left front neck and across Button Band. 98 (98:102) sts.

Work 3 rows in rib as given for Back.

1st buttonhole row Rib 2, cast off 3, rib to end.

2nd buttonhole row Rib to last 2 sts, cast on 3, rib to end.

Rib 4 rows. Cast off in rib.

To Make Up

With DK yarn, embroider flowers and leaves in lazy daisy stitch with french knot (see pages 61, 75) in centre between bobbles of Panel B. Join side and sleeve seams. Set in sleeves. Sew on buttons.

Farmyard Cardigan

SEE PAGE
27

MATERIALS

4 X 50g balls of Hayfield Silky Cotton DK in main colour (A).
Small amounts of same in Black, Grey, Blue, Red, Gold and Green.
1 pair of 4 mm (No 8/US 5) knitting needles.
Medium size crochet hook.
4 buttons.

MEASUREMENTS

To fit age   1 year
All round at chest

70 cm		27½ in

Length to shoulder

31 cm		12¼ in

Sleeve seam 20 cm   8 in

TENSION

22 sts and 28 rows to 10 cm/4 in over st st on 4 mm (No 8/US 5) needles.

ABBREVIATIONS

See page 39.

NOTE

Use a separate length of yarn for each section and twist yarns together on wrong side when changing colour to avoid holes. If preferred, small areas of contrast may be Swiss Darned when knitting is complete.

Back

With 4 mm (No 8/US 5) needles and A, cast on 77 sts.
Beg with a K row and working in st st throughout, cont in patt from chart as indicated for Back, reading K rows from right to left and P rows from left to right, until 46 rows in all have been worked.

Shape armholes

Keeping patt correct, cast off 5 sts at beg of next 2 rows. 67 sts.
Cont without shaping until 84 rows in all have been worked.

Shape shoulders

Cont in A only, cast off 10 sts at beg of next 4 rows. Cast off rem 27 sts.

Left Front

With 4 mm (No 8/US 5) needles and A, cast on 37 sts.
Beg with a K row and working in st st throughout, cont in patt from chart as indicated for Left Front until 44 rows in all have been worked.

Shape front

Keeping patt correct, dec one st at end (front edge) of next row. Patt 1 row.

Shape armhole

Cast off 5 sts at beg of next row. 31 sts.
Keeping armhole edge straight, cont dec one st a front edge on next and every foll 3rd row until 20 sts rem.
Cont without shaping until work measures same as Back to shoulder shaping, ending with a wrong side row.

Shape shoulder

Cont in A only, cast off 10 sts at beg of next row. Work 1 row. Cast off rem 10 sts.

Right Front

Work as given for Left Front, reversing all shaping and working patt from chart as indicated for Right Front.

Sleeves

With 4 mm (No 8/US 5) needles and A, cast on 43 sts.

Beg with a K row and working in st st throughout, cont in patt from chart as indicated for Sleeve, *at the same time*, inc one st at each end of 7th and every foll 6th row until there are 59 sts.

Cont without shaping, completing motifs already started only, work a further 9 rows. With A, work 2 rows. Cast off.

To Make Up

Join shoulder seams. Sew on sleeves, placing centre of sleeves to shoulder seams and sewing last 2 cm/¾ in of row ends of sleeve tops to cast off sts at armholes. Join side and sleeve seams.

Crochet edging

With crochet hook, A, right side facing and beg at Right Front side seam, work 1 row or double crochet (the number of double crochet should be divisible by 3) along cast on edge of Right Front, up Right Front, across back neck, down Left Front, along cast on edge of Left Front and Back, slip stitch in first double crochet.

Next round [2 treble in same double crochet as slip stitch, miss 2 double crochet, slip stitch in next double crochet] to end, making 4 buttonhole loops along straight edge of Right Front by working 3 chain, miss 2 double crochet, slip stitch in next double crochet. Fasten off.

Work edging in same way along cast on edge of sleeves.

Sew on buttons.

If necessary work Swiss Darning. Work embroidery with colour and stitches as indicated on chart. (See diagrams page 70.)

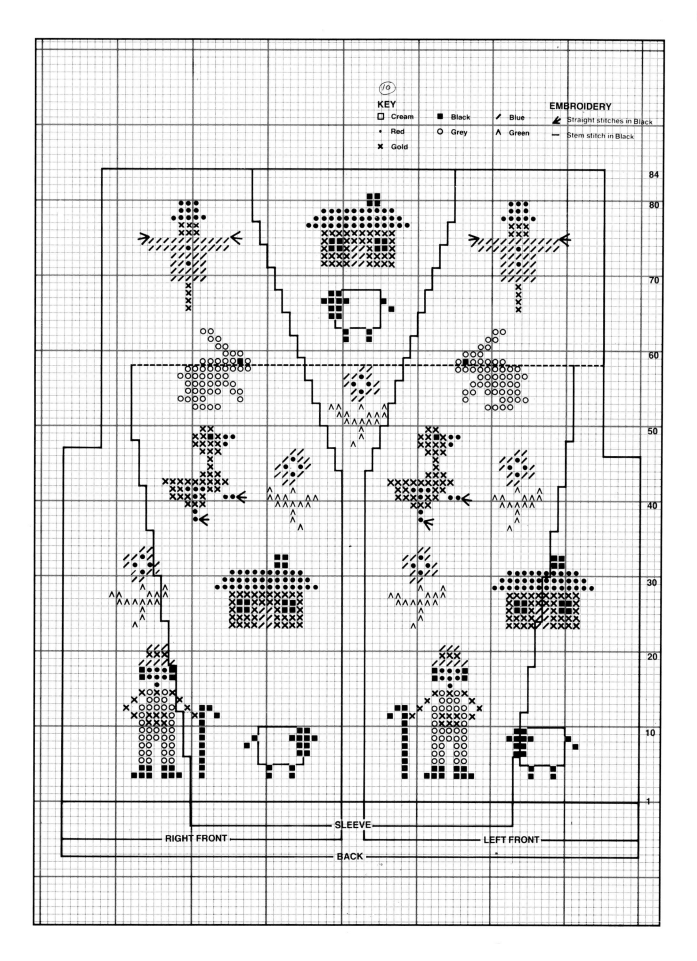

Aran Sweater Dress

SEE PAGE
28

MATERIALS
6 (6:7) 100g balls of Hayfield Brig Aran.
1 pair each of 3¾ mm (No 9/US 4) and
4½ mm (No 7/US 6) knitting needles.
One 3¾ mm (No 9/US 4) circular needle
40 cm long.
Cable needle.

MEASUREMENTS
To fit age
        1 (2:3) years
All round at chest
      64 (72:80) cm   25¼ (28¼:31½) in
Length to shoulder
      38 (44:50) cm   15 (17¼:19¾) in
Sleeve seam
      22 (24:26) cm   8½ (9½:10¼) in

TENSION
19 sts and 25 rows to 10 cm/4 in over st st
using 4½ mm (No 7/US 6) needles.

ABBREVIATIONS
C4F = slip next 2 sts onto cable needle
        and leave at front, K2, then K2
        from cable needle.
C4B = slip next 2 sts onto cable needle
        and leave at back, K2, then K2
        from cable needle.
FC   = slip next 2 sts onto cable needle
        and leave at front, P1, then K2
        from cable needle.
BC   = slip next st onto cable needle
        and leave at back, K2, then P1
        from cable needle.
TW2L = slip next st onto cable needle and
        leave at front, P1, then K1 from
        cable needle.
TW2R = slip next st onto cable needle and
        leave at back, K1, then P1 from
        cable needle.
Also see page 39.

Panel A – worked over 7 sts.
1st row (wrong side) K5, P2.
2nd row FC, P4.
3rd row K4, P2, K1.
4th row K1, FC, P3.
5th row K3, P2, K1, P1.
6th row P1, K1, FC, P2.
7th row K2, P2, K1, P1, K1.
8th row K1, P1, K1, FC, P1.
9th row K1, P2, [K1, P1] twice.
10th row [P1, K1] twice, FC.
11th row P2, K1, [P1, K1] twice.
12th row [K1, P1] twice, BC.
13th row As 9th row.
14th row P1, K1, P1, BC, P1.
15th row As 7th row.
16th row K1, P1, BC, P2.
17th row As 5th row.
18th row P1, BC, P3.
19th row As 3rd row.
20th row BC, P4.
These 20 rows form patt.

Panel B – worked over 10 sts.
1st row (wrong side) K1, P8, K1.
2nd row P1, C4B, C4F, P1.
3rd row As 1st row.
4th row P1, K8, P1.
5th row As 1st row.
6th row P1, C4F, C4B, P1.
7th row As 1st row.
8th row As 4th row.
These 8 rows form patt.

Panel C – worked over 17 sts.
1st row (wrong side) K3, K into front, back,
front, back, front of next st, K2, P2, K1, P2,
K2, K into front, back, front, back, front of
next st, K3.
2nd row P3, K5 tog tbl, P2, slip first 3 sts
onto cable needle and leave at front, K2,
slip first (P) st on cable needle back onto
left-hand needle, P this st, then K2 from
cable needle, P2, K5 tog tbl, P3.
3rd row K6, P2, K1, P2, K6.
4th row P5, BC, P1, FC, P5.
5th row K5, P2, K3, P2, K5.
6th row P4, BC, P3, FC, P4.
7th row K4, P2, K2, K into front, back, front,
back, front of next st, K2, P2, K4.
8th row P3, BC, P2, K5 tog tbl, P2, FC, P3.
9th row K3, P2, K7, P2, K3.
10th row P2, BC, P7, FC, P2.
11th row K2, P2, K2, K into front, back,
front, back, front of next st, K3, K into front,
back, front, back, front of next st, K2, P2,
K2.
12th row P1, BC, P2, K5 tog tbl, P3, K5 tog
tbl, P2, FC, P1.
13th row K1, P2, K11, P2, K1.
14th row P1, K2, P11, K2, P1.
15th row K1, P2, K3, [K into front, back,
front, back, front of next st, K3] twice, P2,
K1.
16th row P1, FC, P2, K5 tog tbl, P3, K5 tog
tbl, P2, BC, P1.
17th row K2, P2, K9, P2, K2.
18th row P2, FC, P7, BC, P2.
19th row K3, P2, K3, K into front, back,
front, back, front of next st, K3, P2, K3.
20th row P3, FC, P2, K5 tog tbl, P2, BC, P3.
21st row K4, P2, K5, P2, K4.
22nd row P4, FC, P3, BC, P4.
23rd row As 5th row.
24th row P5, FC, P1, BC, P5.
These 24 rows form patt.

Panel D – worked over 7 sts.
1st row (wrong side) P2, K5.
2nd row P4, BC.
3rd row K1, P2, K4.
4th row P3, BC, K1.
5th row P1, K1, P2, K3.
6th row P2, BC, K1, P1.
7th row K1, P1, K1, P2, K2.
8th row P1, BC, K1, P1, K1.
9th row [P1, K1] twice, P2, K1.
10th row BC, [K1, P1] twice.
11th row [K1, P1] 3 times, P1.
12th row FC, [P1, K1] twice.
13th row As 9th row.
14th row P1, FC, P1, K1, P1.
15th row As 7th row.
16th row P2, FC, P1, K1.
17th row As 5th row.

18th row P3, FC, P1.
19th row As 3rd row.
20th row P4, FC.
These 20 rows form patt.

Back
With 3¾ mm (No 9/US 4) needles, cast on
82 (87:97) sts.
1st row (right side) K2, [K1, P2, K2] to end.
2nd row P2, [K2, P3] to end.
3rd row K2, [TW2L, P1, K2] to end.
4th row P2, [K1, P1, K1, P2] to end.
5th row K2, [P1, TW2L, K2] to end.
6th row P2, [P1, K2, P2] to end.
7th row K2, [P1, TW2R, K2] to end.
8th row As 4th row.
9th row K2, [TW2R, P1, K2] to end.
10th row As 2nd row.
Rows 3 to 10 form rib patt. Cont in rib patt
until work measures 8 (10:12) cm/3
(4:4¾) in from beg, ending with a right side
row. K 4 rows inc 3 (6:4) sts evenly across
last row. 85 (93:101) sts.
Change to 4½ mm (No 7/US 6) needles.
Work in patt as follows:
1st row (wrong side) K1, [P1, K1] 2 (4:6)
times, work 1st row of Panel A, *K1, P4, K1,
work 1st row of Panel B, K1, P4, K1*, work
1st row of Panel C, rep from * to *, work
1st row of Panel D, K1, [P1, K1] 2 (4:6)
times.
2nd row P1, [K1, P1] 2 (4:6) times, work 2nd
row of Panel D, *P1, K4, P1, work 2nd row of
Panel B, P1, K4, P1*, work 2nd row of Panel
C, rep from * to *, work 2nd row of Panel A,
P1, [K1, P1] 2 (4:6) times.
3rd row P1, [K1, P1] 2 (4:6) times, work 3rd
row of Panel A, *K1, P4, K1, work 3rd row of
Panel B, K1, P4, K1*, work 3rd row of Panel
C, rep from * to *, work 3rd row of Panel D,
P1, [K1, P1] 2 (4:6) times.
4th row K1, [P1, K1] 2 (4:6) times, work 4th
row of Panel D, P1, C4B, P1, work 4th row of
Panel B, P1, C4B, P1, work 4th row of Panel
C, P1, C4F, P1, work 4th row of Panel B, P1,
C4F, P1, work 4th row of Panel A, K1, [P1,
K1] 2 (4:6) times.
These 4 rows set patt. Cont in patt as set,
working appropriate rows of Panels until
work measures 38 (44:50) cm/15 (17¼:
19¾) in from beg, ending with a wrong
side row.
Shape shoulders
Cast off 11 (13:14) sts at beg of next 2 rows
and 12 (13:15) sts at beg of foll 2 rows.
Leave rem 39 (41:43) sts on a holder.

Front
Work as given for Back until work measures
33 (38:44) cm/13 (15:17¼) in from beg,
ending with a wrong side row.
Shape neck
Next row Patt 33 (36:39), turn. Work on this
set of sts only. Keeping patt correct, dec
one st at neck edge on every row until 23
(26:29) sts rem.
Cont without shaping for a few rows until
work measures same as Back to shoulder
shaping, ending at side edge.

Shape shoulder

Cast off 11 (13:14) sts at beg of next row. Work 1 row. Cast off rem 12 (13:15) sts. With right side facing, slip centre 19 (21:23) sts onto a holder, rejoin yarn to rem sts and patt to end. Complete to match first side.

Sleeves

With 3¾ mm (No 9/US 4) needles, cast on 32 (37:42) sts. Work in rib patt as given for Back until work measures 5 (6:6) cm/2 (2¼:2¼) in from beg, ending with a right side row. K 4 rows inc 3 (12:11) sts evenly across last row. 35 (49:53) sts.
Change to 4½ mm (No 7/US 6) needles. Work in patt as follows:

1st size only
1st row (wrong side) K1, P1, K2, P4, K1, work 1st row of Panel C, K1, P4, K2, P1, K1.
2nd row P1, K1, P2, K4, P1, work 2nd row of Panel C, P1, K4, P2, K1, P1.
3rd row [P1, K1] twice, P4, K1, work 3rd row of Panel C, K1, P4, [K1, P1] twice.
4th row [K1, P1] twice, C4B, P1, work 4th row of Panel C, P1, C4F, [P1, K1] twice.

2nd and 3rd sizes only
1st row (wrong side) [K1, P1] (0:1) time, work 1st row of Panel B, K1, P4, K1, work 1st row of Panel C, K1, P4, K1, work 1st row of Panel B, [P1, K1] (0:1) time.
2nd row [P1, K1] (0:1) time, work 2nd row of Panel B, P1, K4, P1, work 2nd row of Panel C, P1, K4, P1, work 2nd row of Panel B, [K1, P1] (0:1) time.
3rd row [P1, K1] (0:1) time, work 3rd row of Panel B, K1, P4, K1, work 3rd row of Panel C, K1, P4, K1, work 3rd row of Panel B, [K1, P1] (0:1) time.
4th row [K1, P1] (0:1) time, work 4th row of Panel B, P1, C4B, P1, work 4th row of Panel C, P1, C4F, P1, work 4th row of Panel B, [P1, K1] (0:1) time.

All sizes
These 4 rows set patt. Cont in patt as set, working appropriate rows of Panels, *at the same time*, inc one st at each end of next and every foll 2nd (2nd:3rd) row until there are 65 (77:81) sts, working inc sts into double moss st (side edge) patt.
Cont without shaping until work measures 22 (24:26) cm/8½ (9½:10¼) in from beg, ending with a wrong side row. Cast off.

Neckband

Join shoulder seams.
With 3¾ mm (No 9/US 4) circular needle, right side facing and beg at left shoulder seam, pick up and K 17 (21:21) sts down left front neck, K across 19 (21:23) sts at centre front, pick up and K 17 (21:21) sts up right front neck, K across 39 (41:43) sts at back neck. 92 (104:108) sts. Work in rounds of K2, P2 rib for 5 (6:7) cm/2 (2¼:2¾) in. K 5 rounds. Cast off loosely.

To Make Up

Sew on sleeves, placing centre of sleeves to shoulder seams. Join side and sleeve seams.

Aran Coat with Large Collar

SEE PAGE
29

MATERIALS

10 (11) 50g balls of Hayfield Pure Wool Classics DK or 7 (8) 50g balls of Hayfield Grampian DK.
1 pair each of 3¼ mm (No 10/US 3) and 4 mm (No 8/US 5) knitting needles.
Cable needle.
5 (6) buttons.

MEASUREMENTS

To fit age	2 (3) years	
All round at chest		
	68 (74) cm	26¾ (29) in
Length to shoulder		
	42 (48) cm	16½ (19) in
Sleeve seam	22 (25) cm	8¾ (10) in

TENSION

22sts and 28 rows to 10 cm/4 in over st st on 4 mm (No 8/US 5) needles.

ABBREVIATIONS

C4B = slip next 2 sts onto cable needle and leave at back, K2, then K2 from cable needle.
C4F = slip next 2 sts onto cable needle and leave at front, K2, then K2 from cable needle.
BC = slip next st onto cable needle and leave at back, K2, then P1 from cable needle.
FC = slip next 2 sts onto cable needle and leave at front, P1, then K2 from cable needle.
Also see page 39.

Panel A – worked over 6 sts.
1st and foll alt row (wrong side) K1, P4, K1.
2nd row P1, K4, P1.
4th row P1, C4B, P1.
These 4 rows form patt.

Panel B – worked over 10 sts.
1st row and every foll alt rows (wrong side) K1, P8, K1.
2nd row P1, C4B, C4F, P1.
4th row P1, K8, P1.
6th row P1, C4F, C4B, P1.
8th row As 4th row.
These 8 rows form patt.

Panel C – worked over 20 sts.
1st row (wrong side) K3, P2, K3, P4, K3, P2, K3.
2nd row [P2, BC] twice, [FC, P2] twice.
3rd row [K2, P2, K3, P2] twice, K2.
4th row P1, [BC, P2] twice, FC, P2, FC, P1.
5th row K1, P2, K3, P2, K4, P2, K3, P2, K1.
6th row [BC, P2] twice, pick up loop lying between sts and [K1, P1, K1, P1, K1] into it, turn, P5, turn, K5, turn, P2 tog, P1, P2 tog, turn, slip 1, K2 tog, psso, P1 then pass bobble st over first st, P1, FC, P2, FC.
7th row [P2, K3] twice, [K3, P2] twice.
8th row [FC, P2] twice, [P2, BC] twice.

9th row As 5th row.
10th row P1, [FC, P2] twice, BC, P2, BC, P1.
11th row As 3rd row.
12th row [P2, FC] twice, [BC, P2] twice.
These 12 rows form patt.

Panel D – worked over 6 sts.
1st row and foll alt row (wrong side) K1, P4, K1.
2nd row P1, K4, P1.
4th row P1, C4F, P1.
These 4 rows form patt.

Back

With 4 mm (No 8/US 5) needles, cast on 93 (101) sts.
1st row (right side) K1, [P1, K1] to end.
2nd row P1, [K1, P1] to end.
Rep these 2 rows until work measures 3 cm/1¼ in from beg, ending with a right side row and inc 15 sts evenly across last row. 108 (116) sts.
Work in patt as follows:
1st row (wrong side) K1 (5), work 1st row of Panels A, B, A, C, A, B, D, C, D, B and D, K1 (5).
2nd row P1 (5), work 2nd row of Panels D, B, D, C, D, B, A, C, A, B and A, P1 (5).
These 2 rows set patt. Cont in patt as set, working appropriate rows of Panels until work measures 42 (48) cm/16½ (19) in from beg, ending with a wrong side row.
Shape shoulders
Cast off 18 (19) sts at beg of next 2 rows and 18 (20) sts at beg of foll 2 rows. Cast off rem 36 (38) sts.

Left Front

With 4 mm (No 8/US 5) needles, cast on 43 (47) sts.
Work in rib as given for Back for 3 cm/1¼ in, ending with a right side row and inc 7 sts evenly across last row. 50 (54) sts.
Work in patt as follows:
1st row (wrong side) K1, work 1st row of Panels D, C, D, B and D, K1 (5).
2nd row P1 (5), work 2nd row of Panels D, B, D, C and D, P1.
These 2 rows set patt. Cont in patt as set, working appropriate rows of Panels until work measures 29 (35) cm/11¼ (13¾) in from beg, ending with a wrong side row.
Shape front
Keeping patt correct, dec one st at end (front edge) of next and 9 foll alt rows, then at same edge on every 3rd row until 36 (39) sts rem.
Cont without shaping until work measures same as Back to shoulder shaping, ending with a wrong side row.
Shape shoulder
Cast of 18 (19) sts at beg of next row. Work 1 row. Cast off rem 18 (20) sts.

continued overleaf

Right Front

Work as given for Left Front, reversing all shaping and placing patt as follows:
1st row (wrong side) K1 (5), work 1st row of Panels A, B, A, C and A, K1.
2nd row P1, work 2nd row of Panels A, C, A, B and A, P1 (5).

Sleeves

With 3¼ mm (No 10/US 3) needles, cast on 43 sts.
Work in rib as given for Back for 5 cm/2 in, ending with a wrong side row.
Next row Inc in each of next 3 sts, [rib 1, inc in each of next 3 sts] to end. 76 sts.
Change to 4 mm (No 8/US 5) needles.
Work in patt as follows:
1st row (wrong side) K1, work 1st row of Panels A, C, A, B, D, C and D, K1.
2nd row P1, work 2nd row of Panels D, C, D, B, A, C and A, P1.
These 2 rows set patt. Cont in patt as set, working appropriate rows of Panels, *at the same time,* inc one st at each end of every foll 8th (6th) row until there are 84 (90) sts, working inc sts into reverse st st.
Cont without shaping until work measures 22 (25) cm/8¾ (10) in from beg, ending with a wrong side row. Cast off.

Buttonhole Band

With 3¼ mm (No 10/US 3) needles and right side facing, pick up and K 67 (81) sts evenly along straight edge of Right Front to beg of shaping. Beg with a 2nd row, work 3 rows in rib as given for Back.
1st buttonhole row Rib 2, [cast off 2, rib 12 sts more] 4 (5) times, cast off 2, rib to end.
2nd buttonhole row Rib to end, casting on 2 sts over those cast off in previous row.
Rib 4 rows. Cast off in rib.

Button Band

Work to match Buttonhole Band, omitting buttonholes.

Collar

With 4 mm (No 8/US 5) needles, cast on 3 sts for left half of collar.
Next row (right side) P1, K2.
Next row Cast on 3, work 1st row of Panel D.
Next row Work 2nd row of Panel D.
Next row Cast on 3, K3 (part of 1st row of Panel C), work 3rd row of Panel D.
Next row Work 4th row of Panel D, P2, inc in next st.
Inc one st at beg (inside edge) of next row and at same edge on every row until there are 42 sts, working inc sts into Panel C, D and B.
Cont without shaping for a few rows until work fits along shaped edge of Left Front, ending with a 1st row of Panel C.
Shape collar
Next row Patt 8, turn.
Next row and 6 foll alt rows Slip 1, patt to end.
Next row Patt 25, turn.
Next row Patt 33, turn.
Next row Patt 42.
Next row Patt 33, turn.
Next row Patt 25, turn.
Next row Patt 8, turn.
Patt 1 row, thus ending at inside edge.
Cast on 4 sts at beg of next and 2 foll alt rows, working cast on sts into Panels D and C. 54 sts.** Patt 1 row. Leave these sts on a spare needle.
With 4 mm (No 8/US 5) needles, cast on 3 sts for right half of collar.
Next row (right side) K2, P1.
Next row K1, P2.
Next row Cast on 3, work 2nd row of Panel A.

Next row Work 3rd row of Panel A.
Next row Cast on 3, P3, (part of 2nd row of Panel C), work 4th row of Panel A.
Next row Work 1st row of Panel A, K3, inc in last st.
Work as given for left half of collar to**, but working Panel A instead of Panel D and ending with a 2nd row of Panel C before collar shaping.
Next row Patt 54, cast on 8, then patt across sts of left half of collar. 116 sts.
Cont in patt across all sts, work 16 rows.
Shape point
Cast off 3 sts at beg of every row until 2 sts rem. K2 tog. Fasten off.

Collar Edgings

With 3¼ mm (No 10/US 3) needles and right side facing, pick up and K 59 sts along straight outside edge of left half of collar and 52 sts along shaped edge to point, turn. 111 sts.
Work in rib as given for Back for 4 rows, inc one st at beg of every row. Cast off in rib.
Work other side to match.

To Make Up

Join shoulder seams. Sew on sleeves, placing centre of sleeves to shoulder seams. Join side and sleeve seams. Sew collar in place, beg and ending at centre of front bands. Join row ends of collar edging at point.
Make 2 pompons and cord 10 cm long. Attach 1 pompon to each end of cord. Sew to point of collar, letting 1 pompon hang. Sew on buttons.

Sheep Boots

SEE PAGE
2

MATERIALS

1 × 50g ball of Hayfield Pure Wool Classics 4 ply in main colour (M).
Small amount of same in 2 contrast colours (A and B).
1 pair each of 2¾ mm (No 12/US 1) and 3¼ mm (No 10/US 3) knitting needles.

ABBREVIATIONS

See page 39.

To Make

With 2¾ mm (No 12/US 1) needles and M, cast on 53 sts. K 11 rows.
1st row (right side) K1, [P1, K1] to end.
2nd row P1, [K1, P1] to end.
Rep last 2 rows 3 times more.
Next row Rib 3, [P2 tog, yrn, rib 3, K2 tog, yf, rib 3] to end. Rib 5 rows.

Shape instep
Next row K20 M, 13A, turn.
Next row K13A, turn.
K 22 rows in A on these 13 sts. Break off yarn. Leave these sts on a holder.
With right side facing and M, pick up and K 12 sts evenly along side edge of instep, K13 sts from holder, then pick up and K12 sts evenly along other side edge of instep, K rem sts. 77 sts. Cont in M only, K 17 rows. Beg with a K row, work 9 rows in st st.
Next row [P next st tog with corresponding st 9 rows below] to end.
K 13 rows. Cast off.
Join back seam, reversing seam on cuff to allow for turning. Join under seam folding knitting carefully to lie flat to form mitred corners. With M, make cord approximately 40 cm/15¾ in long and thread through holes.**

Ears

With 3¼ mm (No 10/US 3) needles and A, cast on 3 sts for outer ear. Work in garter st (every row K), inc one st at each end of 3rd and foll alt row. 7 sts. Cont straight until work measures 5 cm/2 in from beg. Cast off. Make one more in A and 2 more for inner ear in B. Join paired pieces together. Fold cast off edges in half and sew through all thicknesses to each side of boot.

Tail

With 3¼ mm (No 10/US 3) needles and A, cast on 5 sts, work in st st for 4 cm/1½ in. Cast off. Fold lengthwise and join seam. Sew to back of bootee.
Make another boot, reversing colours on main part and cord.

Mexican Jacket

SEE PAGE
31

MATERIALS

3 (3:4) 50g balls of Hayfield Pure Wool Classics DK or 3 × 50g balls of Hayfield Grampian DK in main colour (M).
Small amount of same in 5 colours (A, B, C, D and E).
1 pair each of 3¼ mm (No 10/US 3) and 4 mm (No 8/US 5) knitting needles.

MEASUREMENTS

To fit age
    6–12 (12–24:24–36) months
All round at chest
    62 (66:70) cm   24½ (26:27½) in
Length to shoulder
    25 (28:32) cm   10 (11:12½) in
Sleeve seam
    16 (22:25) cm   6¼ (8½:10) in

TENSION

22 sts and 28 rows to 10 cm/4 in over st st on 4 mm (No 8/US 5) needles.

NOTE

Use a separate length of yarn for each motif and twist yarns together on wrong side when changing colour to avoid holes. If preferred, motifs may be Swiss Darned when knitting is complete.

Back

With 4 mm (No 8/US 5) needles and M, cast on 69 (73:77) sts.
1st row K1, [P1, K1] to end.
This row forms moss st. Moss st 3 more rows.
Next row K1M, [1A, 1M] to end.
Next row P1A, [1M, 1A] to end.
Cont in st st and M only until work measures 25 (28:32) cm/10 (11:12½) in from beg, ending with a wrong side row.
Shape shoulders
Cast off 10 (11:11) sts at beg of next 2 rows and 11 (11:12) sts at beg of foll 2 rows. Leave rem 27 (29:31) sts on a holder.

Left Front

With 4 mm (No 8/US 5) needles and M, cast on 35 (37:39) sts.
Work 4 rows in moss st as given for Back.
Next row (right side) K1 M, [1A, 1M] to last 4 sts, with M, moss st 4.
Next row With M, moss st 4, P1A, [1M, 1A] to end.
Cont in M only.
Next row K to last 4 sts, moss st 4.
Next row Moss st 4, P to end.
Rep last 2 rows until work measures 15 (17:20) cm/6 (6¾:8) in from beg, ending with a wrong side row.
Work patt from chart 1, reading K rows from right to left and P rows from left to right, as follows:
1st row With M, K13 (14:15), K across 1st row of chart 1, with M, K to last 4 sts, moss st 4.
2nd row With M, moss st 4, P11 (12:13), P across 2nd row of chart 1, with M, P to end.

3rd to 8th row Rep 1st and 2nd rows 3 times more, but working 3rd to 8th rows of chart 1.
Keeping the 4 sts at front edge in moss st and remainder in st st, cont in M only until work measures 20 (23:27) cm/8 (9:10½) in from beg, ending with a right side row.
Shape neck
Cast off 4 (5:6) sts at beg of next row and 3 sts at beg of foll alt row. Dec one st at neck edge on every row until 21 (22:23) sts rem. Cont without shaping until work measures same as Back to shoulder shaping, ending with a wrong side row.
Shape shoulder
Cast off 10 (11:11) sts at beg of next row. Work 1 row. Cast off rem 11 (11:12) sts.

Right Front

With 4 mm (No 8/US 5) needles and M, cast on 35 (37:39) sts.
Work 4 rows in moss st as given for Back.
Next row (right side) With M, moss st 4,

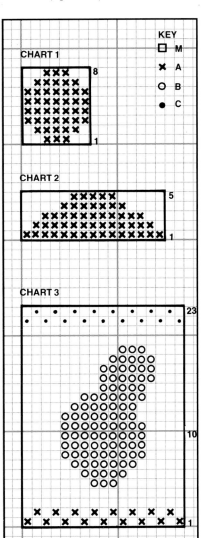

KEY
□ M
✕ A
○ B
● C

CHART 1

CHART 2

CHART 3

K1M, [1A, 1M] to end.
Next row P1 A, [1M, 1A] to last 4 sts, with M, moss st 4.
Cont in M only.
Next row Moss st 4, K to end.
Next row P to last 4 sts, moss st 4.
Complete as Left Front, reversing all shaping and working patt from chart 1 as follows:
1st row With M, moss st 4, K11 (12:13), K across 1st row of chart 1, with M, K to end.
2nd row With M, P13 (14:15), P across 2nd row of chart 1, with M, P to last 4 sts, moss st 4.

Sleeves

With 4 mm (No 8/US 5) needles and M, cast on 33 (35:37) sts. Work 4 rows in moss st as given for Back.
Next row K1C, [1M, 1C] to end.
Next row With M, P twice in first st, [P1C, 1M] to last 2 sts, P1C, with M, P twice in last st.
With M, work 2 rows in st st.
Work patt from chart 2 as follows:
1st row With M, K twice in first st, K9 (10:11), K across 1st row of chart 2, with M, K to last st, K twice in last st.
2nd row With M, P11 (12:13), P across 2nd row of chart 2, with M, P to end.
These 2 rows set patt from chart 2. Work a further 3 rows as set, inc one st at each end of 2nd row. 39 (41:43) sts.
Cont in st st and M only, inc one st at each end of 2nd and every foll 3rd (4th:5th) row until there are 57 (61:65) sts.
Cont without shaping for a few rows until work measures 16 (22:25) cm/6¼ (8½: 10) in from beg, ending with a P row. Cast off.

Pockets

With 4 mm (No 8/US 5) needles and M, cast on 23 sts.
1st row With M, K1, P1, K1, K across 1st row of chart 3, with M, K1, P1, K1.
2nd row With M, K1, P1, K1, P across 2nd row of chart 3, with M, K1, P1, K1.
3rd to 23rd rows Rep last 2 rows 10 times more then work 1st row again, but working 3rd to 23rd row of chart 3. Cont in M only, P 1 row, then work 4 rows in moss st. Cast off.
Make another pocket, reversing patt from chart 3 by reading K rows from left to right and P rows from right to left.

Neckband

Join shoulder seams.
With 3¼ mm (No 10/US 3) needles, M and right side facing, pick up and K 23 sts up right front neck, K across 27 (29:31) sts on back neck, pick up and K 23 sts down left front neck. 73 (75:77) sts.
Work 4 rows in moss st. Cast off, working 2 sts tog at beg and end.

continued overleaf

To Make Up

Sew on sleeves, placing centre of sleeves to shoulder seams. Join side and sleeve seams. If necessary, work Swiss Darning (see diagram page 61).
Embroider cactus flowers in E and lazy daisy stitch (see diagram page 61) and spikes in D and straight stitches (see diagram below).
Embroider sunrays in A and straight stitches. With D, work cross stitches around outside edges of each pocket, omitting cast on edge. Sew on pockets.
Now work cross stitch with D along cast on edge of Right Front, up straight edge, around neck edge, down Left Front, along cast on edge of Left Front and Back. Work cross stitch with D along cast on edge of each sleeve.

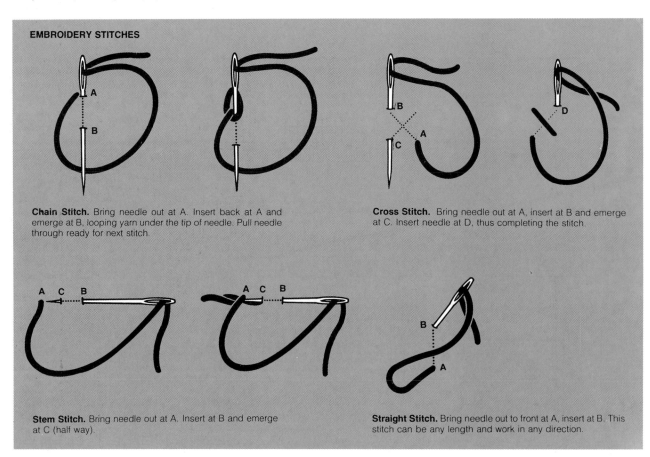

EMBROIDERY STITCHES

Chain Stitch. Bring needle out at A. Insert back at A and emerge at B, looping yarn under the tip of needle. Pull needle through ready for next stitch.

Cross Stitch. Bring needle out at A, insert at B and emerge at C. Insert needle at D, thus completing the stitch.

Stem Stitch. Bring needle out at A. Insert at B and emerge at C (half way).

Straight Stitch. Bring needle out to front at A, insert at B. This stitch can be any length and work in any direction.

Nursery Sweater

SEE PAGE
30

MATERIALS

4 (5) 50g balls of Hayfield Pure Wool Classics DK in main colour (M).
Small amounts of any Hayfield DK yarn in 10 contrast colours (see chart for shades).
1 pair each of 3¼ mm (No 10/US 3) and 4 mm (No 8/US 5) knitting needles.

MEASUREMENTS

To fit age
18–24 (36) months	

All round at chest
65 (76) cm	25½ (30) in

Length to shoulder
36 (41) cm	14 (16) in

Sleeve seam
23 (25) cm	9 (10) in

TENSION

22 sts and 28 rows to 10 cm/4 in over st st on 4 mm (No 8/US 5) needles.

ABBREVIATIONS

See page 39.

NOTE

Use separate length of yarn for each motif and twist yarns together on wrong side when changing colour to avoid holes. If preferred, small areas of contrast may be Swiss Darned when knitting is complete.

Back

With 3¼ mm (No 10/US 3) needles and M, cast on 70 (82) sts.
Work in K1, P1 rib for 4 cm/1½ in, inc one st at each end of last row. 72 (84) sts.
Change to 4 mm (No 8/US 5) needles.
Beg with a K row and working in st st throughout, work 13th (1st) to 104th row of chart 1, reading K (right side) rows from right to left and P rows from left to right.
Cont in M only.

Shape shoulders
Cast off 18 (23) sts at beg of next 2 rows.
Leave rem 36 (38) sts on a holder.

Front

Work as given for Back until 88th row of chart 1 has been worked.
Shape neck
Next row Patt 29 (35), turn.
Work on this set of sts only.
Cast off 4 sts at beg of next row, 2 (3) sts at beg of foll alt row, then 2 sts at beg of foll alt row. Dec one st at neck edge on 3 foll alt rows. Patt 4 rows straight. With M, cast off rem 18 (23) sts.
With right side facing, slip centre 14 sts onto a holder, join yarn to rem sts and patt 2 rows. Complete to match first side.

continued overleaf

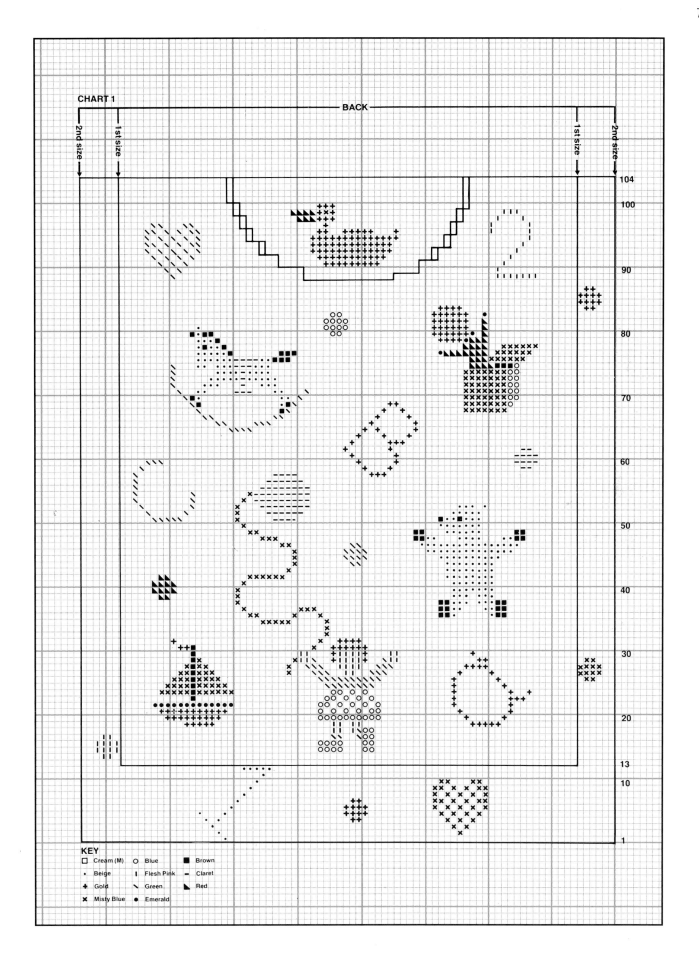

CHART 1

BACK

2nd size
1st size
1st size
2nd size

104
100
90
80
70
60
50
40
30
20
13
10
1

KEY

☐ Cream (M)	○ Blue	■ Brown
• Beige	❘ Flesh Pink	— Claret
+ Gold	\ Green	◣ Red
✕ Misty Blue	● Emerald	

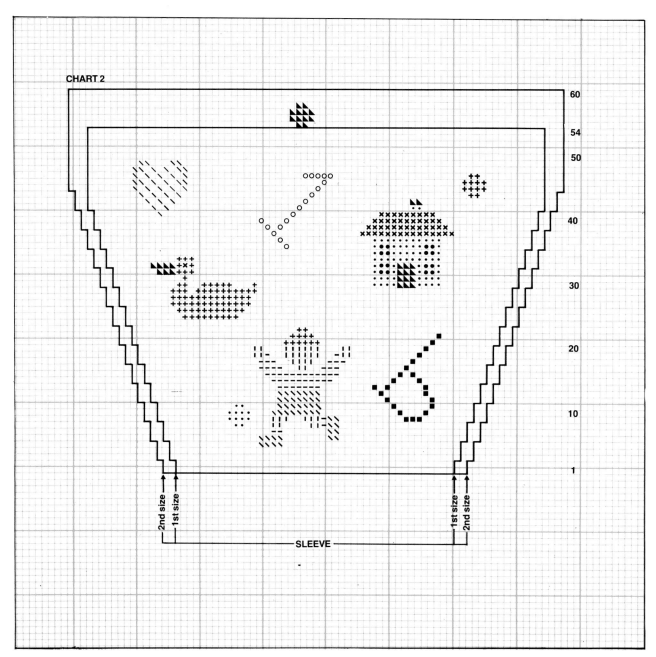

CHART 2

SLEEVE

Sleeves

With 3¼ mm (No 10/US 3) needles and M, cast on 42 (46) sts. Work in K1, P1 rib for 4 cm/1½ in, inc one st at each end of last row. 44 (48) sts.

Change to 4 mm (No 8/US 5) needles.

Beg with a K row and working in st st throughout, work in patt from chart 2, *at the same time*, inc one st at each end of every 3rd row until there are 72 (78) sts.

Cont in patt without shaping until 54th (60th) row of chart 2 has been worked. With M, cast off.

Neckband

Join right shoulder seam.

With 3¼ mm (No 10/US 3) needles, M and right side facing, pick up and K 20 (21) sts down left front neck, K across 14 sts at centre front, pick up and K 20 (21) sts up

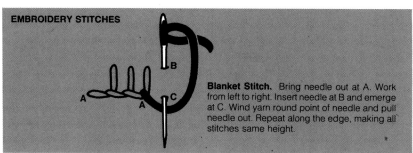

EMBROIDERY STITCHES

Blanket Stitch. Bring needle out at A. Work from left to right. Insert needle at B and emerge at C. Wind yarn round point of needle and pull needle out. Repeat along the edge, making all stitches same height.

right front neck and K across 36 (38) sts at back neck. 90 (94) sts.

Work 9 rows in K1, P1 rib. Cast off in rib.

To Make Up

Work Swiss Darning if necessary (see diagram page 61).

Embroider faces and bow in girl's hair.

Join left shoulder and neckband seam.

Sew on sleeves, placing centre of sleeves to shoulder seams.

Join side and sleeve seams.

With Green, work blanket stitch (see diagram) along all ribbed edges.

Duck Sweater and Pants

SEE PAGE
32

MATERIALS

Sweater : 3 (3) 50g balls of Hayfield Raw Cotton Classics 4 ply in main colour (M).
1 ball of same in first colour (A).
Small amounts of same in second colour (B).
Oddment in third colour (C) for embroidery.
1 pair each of 2¾ mm (No 12/US 1) and 3¼ mm (No 10/US 3) knitting needles.
2 buttons.

Pants : 2 × 50g balls of Hayfield Raw Cotton Classics 4 ply in main colour (M).
1 ball of same in contrast colour (C).
1 pair each of 2¾ mm (No 12/US 1), 3 mm (No 11/US 2) and 3¼ mm (No 10/US 3) knitting needles.
Length of 1.5 cm/½ in wide elastic for waist.

MEASUREMENTS

To fit age

3–6 (6–12) months	
All round at chest	
55 (60) cm	21½ (23½) in
Length to shoulder	
26 (29) cm	10¼ (11½) in
Sleeve seam	
14 (16) cm	5½ (6¼) in
All round at hips	
52 (61) cm	20½ (24) in
Length	
29 (37) cm	11½ (14½) in
Inside leg	
8 (10) cm	3 (4) in

TENSION

28 sts and 36 rows to 10 cm/4 in over st st using 3¼ mm (No 10/US 3) needles.

ABBREVIATIONS

See page 39.

NOTE

Use a separate length of yarn for each motif and twist yarns together on wrong side when changing colour to avoid holes.

Sweater

Back

With 2¾ mm (No 12/US 1) needles and M, cast on 74 (82) sts.
1st row (right side) K2, [P2, K2] to end.
2nd row P2, [K2, P2] to end.
Rep these 2 rows until work measures 4 cm/1½ in from beg, ending with a wrong side row and inc 3 sts evenly across last row. 77 (85) sts.
Change to 3¼ mm (No 10/US 3) needles.
Beg with a K row, work 4 rows in st st.
Reading K rows from right to left and P rows from left to right, work border patt from chart as follows:
1st row K10 (12) M, [work across 13 sts of 1st row of chart, 9 (11) M] 3 times, 1M.
2nd row P10 (12) M, [work across 13 sts of

2nd row of chart, 9 (11) M] 3 times, 1M.
3rd to 19th rows Rep 1st and 2nd rows 8 times more then work 1st row again but working 3rd to 19th rows of chart.**
Beg with a P row, cont in st st and M only until work measures 26 (29) cm/10¼ (11½) in from beg, ending with a P row.
Shape shoulders
Cast off 13 (14) sts at beg of next 2 rows and 12 (13) sts at beg of foll 2 rows. Leave rem 27 (31) sts on a holder.

Front

Work as given for Back to **. Now cont in st st and M only until work measures 18 (19) cm/7 (7½) in from beg, ending with a P row.
Divide for opening
Next row K35 (39), cast off 7, K to end.
Cont on last set of sts only until work measures 23 (25) cm/9 (10) in from beg, ending with a P row.
Shape neck
Cast off 3 sts at beg of next row. Dec one st at neck edge on every row until 25 (27) sts rem.
Cont without shaping for a few rows until work measures same as Back to shoulder shaping, ending with a K row.
Shape shoulder
Cast off 13 (14) sts at beg of next row. Work 1 row. Cast off rem 12 (13) sts.
With wrong side facing, rejoin yarn to rem sts and P to end. Complete to match first side, reversing all shaping.

Sleeves

With 2¾ mm (No 12/US 1) needles and M, cast on 34 (38) sts.

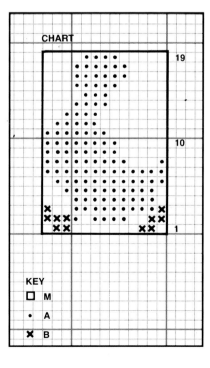

CHART

KEY
☐ M
• A
✗ B

Work 3 cm/1¼ in in rib as given for Back welt, ending with a wrong side row and inc 6 sts evenly across last row. 40 (44) sts.
Change to 3¼ mm (No 10/US 3) needles.
Beg K row, cont in st st, inc one st at each end of every foll alt row until there are 62 (70) sts.
Cont without shaping until work measures 11 (13) cm/4¼ (5) in, ending with a P row.
Now work 3 cm/1¼ in in rib as given for Back welt, ending with a wrong side row.
Cast off in rib.

Buttonhole Band

With 2¾ mm (No 12/US 1) needles, right side facing and M, pick up and K 14 (18) sts evenly along right front edge of opening for girl or left front edge of opening for boy.
Beg with a 2nd row, work 3 rows in rib as given for Back welt.
1st buttonhole row (right side) Rib 3, cast off 2, rib to last 5 sts, cast off 2, rib to end.
2nd buttonhole row Rib to end, casting on 2 sts over those cast off in previous row.
Rib a further 3 rows. Cast off in rib.

Button Band

With 2¾ mm (No 12/US 1) needles, right side facing and M, pick up and K 14 (18) sts evenly along left front edge of opening for girl or right front edge of opening for boy. Beg with a 2nd row, work 8 rows in rib as given for Back welt. Cast off in rib.

Collar

Join shoulder seams.
With 2¾ mm (No 12/US 1) needles, right side facing, M and beg at centre of buttonhole band for girl or button band for boy, pick up and K 23 (24) sts up right front neck, work across back neck sts as follows: [K1, K twice in next st] 13 (15) times, K1, pick up and K 23 (24) sts down left front neck to centre of button band for girl or buttonhole band for boy. 86 (94) sts.
Beg with a 2nd row, work 7 cm/2¾ in in rib as given for Back welt. Cast off loosely in rib.

To Make Up

Lap buttonhole band over button band, then catch down lower ends to cast off sts at base of opening. Sew on sleeves, placing centre of sleeves to shoulder seams. Beg at top of welt, join side then sleeve seams. Sew on buttons.
Embroider beak on each duck in B and bow around neck of each duck with C.

Pants

Back and Front Alike

With 3 mm (No 11/US 2) needles and M, cast on 62 (74) sts.
Beg with a K row, cont in st st until work

continued overleaf

measures 3 cm/1¼ in from beg, ending with a P row. Change to C and work 6 rows, inc 12 sts evenly across last row. 74 (86) sts.
Change to 3¼ mm (No 10/US 3) needles. Work in st st and stripe patt of 2 rows M and 6 rows C throughout, cont until work measures 24 (30) cm/9½ (11¾) in from beg, ending with a P row.
Divide for leg
Next row Patt 35 (41), K2 tog, turn.

Work on first set of sts only. Work 1 row. Dec one st at end of next and every foll alt row until 33 (36) sts rem then at same edge on 2 (3) foll 3rd rows. 31 (33) sts.
Cont without shaping for a few rows until work measures 29 (37) cm/11½ (14½) in from beg, ending with a P row. Cont in M only, K 1 row.
Change to 2¾ mm (No 12/US 1) needles.
1st row K1, [P1, K1] to end.
2nd row P1, [K1, P1] to end.

Rep last 2 rows 3 times more then work 1st row again. Cast off in rib.
With right side facing, join yarn to rem sts, K2 tog, patt to end. Complete to match first side, reversing shaping.

To Make Up
Join side and inside leg seams. Join elastic to form ring. Fold first 3 cm/1¼ in from cast on edge to inside for waist band. Insert elastic, then slip stitch waist band in place.

Bee Cardigan, Bootees and Beanie Hat

SEE PAGE
33

MATERIALS
Cardigan : 2 (2:3) 50g balls of Hayfield Pure Wool Classics 4 ply in main colour (M).
Bootees : 1 ball of Hayfield Pure Woold Classics 4 ply in main colour.
Hat : 1 × 50g ball of Hayfield Grampian 4 ply.
Oddments in Yellow and Black for embroidery for Cardigan and Bootees.
1 pair each of 2¾ mm (No 12/US 1) and 3¼ mm (No 10/US 3) knitting needles.
Medium size crochet hook.
5 buttons for cardigan and 2 buttons for bootees.

MEASUREMENTS
To fit age
        3 (6:9) months
All round at chest
        50 (52:55) cm   19½ (20½:21½) in
Length to shoulder
        24 (26:29) cm   9½ (10¼:11½) in
Sleeve seam
        12 (13:15) cm   4¾ (5:6) in

TENSION
28 sts and 36 rows to 10 cm/4 in over st st on 3¼ mm (No 10/US 3) needles.

ABBREVIATIONS
See page 39.

Cardigan

Back
With 2¾ mm (No 12/US 1) needles and M, cast on 70 (74:78) sts. Work in K1, P1 rib for 5 cm/2 in.
Change to 3¼ mm (No 10/US 3) needles. Beg with a K row, cont in st st until work measures 12 (13:15) cm/4¾ (5:6) in from beg, ending with a P row.
Shape raglan armholes
Next row K1, K2 tog tbl, K to last 3 sts, K2 tog, K1.
Next row P.
Rep last 2 rows until 34 (36:36) sts rem, ending with a P row. Cast off.

Left Front
With 2¾ mm (No 12/US 1) needles and M, cast on 41 (43:45) sts.
1st row (right side) K1, [P1, K1] to last 6 sts, K6.
2nd row K6, P1, [K1, P1] to end.
Rep last 2 rows until work measures 5 cm/2 in from beg, ending with a wrong side row.
Change to 3¼ mm (No 10/US 3) needles.
Next row K to end.
Next row K6, P to end.
Rep last 2 rows until work measures 12 (13:15) cm/4¾ (5:6) in from beg, ending with a wrong side row.
Shape raglan armhole
Next row K1, K2 tog tbl, K to end.
Next row K6, P to end.
Rep last 2 rows until 25 (26:26) sts rem, ending with a dec row.
Shape neck
Cast off 20 (21:21) sts at beg of next row.
Next row K1, K2 tog tbl, K2 tog. P 1 row.
Next row K1, K2 tog. P 1 row.
K 2 tog and fasten off.

Right Front
With 2¾ mm (No 12/US 1) needles and M, cast on 41 (43:45) sts.
1st row (right side) K6, [K1, P1] to last st, K1.
2nd row P1, [K1, P1] to last 6 sts, P6.
Rep last 2 rows until work measures 5 cm/2 in from beg, ending with a wrong side row.
Change to 3¼ mm (No 10/US 3) needles.
Beg with a K row, cont in st st until work measures 12 (13:15) cm/4¾ (5:6) in from beg, ending with a P row.
Shape raglan armhole
Next row K to last 3 sts, K2 tog, K1.
Next row P.
Rep last 2 rows until 26 (27:27) sts rem, ending with a P row.
Shape neck
Next row Cast off 20 (21:21), K to last 3 sts, K2 tog, K1. P 1 row.
Next row [K2 tog] twice, K1. P 1 row.
Next row K2 tog, K1. P 1 row.
K 2 tog and fasten off.

Sleeves
With 3¼ mm (No 10/US 3) needles and M, cast on 40 (44:48) sts.
Beg with a K row, work 12 rows in st st dec one st at each end of 3rd and foll 6th row.
Next row [K4, K2 tog, K3 (4:5) sts] to end. 32 (36:40) sts.
Change to 2¾ mm (No 12/US 1) needles and work 3 rows in K1, P1 rib.
Next row [Rib 4, inc in next st, rib 3 (4:5) sts] to end. 36 (40:44) sts.
Change to 3¼ mm (No 10/US 3) needles. Beg with a K row, cont in st st inc one st at each end of 3rd and every foll 4th (5th:6th) row until there are 50 (54:58) sts.
Cont without shaping until work measures 12 (13:15) cm/4¾ (5:6) in from beg of rib, ending with a P row.
Shape raglan top
Next row K1, K2 tog tbl, K to last 3 sts, K2 tog, K1.
Next row P.
Rep last 2 rows until 14 (16:16) sts rem, ending with a P row. Cast off.

Right Front Band
With 3¼ mm (No 10/US 3) needles and M, cast on 8 sts.
Work in st st until band when slightly stretched fits up Right Front to beg of neck shaping. Cast off.
With crochet hook, M and right side facing, work picot edging along long straight edge of band as follows: [1 double crochet into next st, 3 chain, slip st in 3rd chain from hook] to end.
Work other side in same way. Place band on top of last few sts at front edge of Right Front and sew in place.

Collar
Join all raglan seams.
With 3¼ mm (No 10/US 3) needles, M and right side facing, pick up and K 54 (58:58) sts evenly around neck edge, omitting front bands.
Beg with a K row, work 2 rows in st st.
Next row K1, inc in next st, K to last 2 sts, inc in next st, K1.
Next row P.

Rep last 2 rows 4 times more. Work 2 rows straight. Cast off.
Work picot edging around collar as given for Right Front Band.

To Make Up

Work picot edging along cast on edge of Sleeves. Join side and sleeve seams, reversing seams on cuffs. Turn back cuffs. Make 5 buttonholes by pushing thick needle through 2 thicknesses of Right Front Band, first one 1 cm/¼ in up from cast on edge and last one 1 cm/ ¼ in down from cast off edge and rem 3 evenly spaced between. Neaten buttonholes. With Yellow and Black, embroider bees along Right Front Band, on each corner of Collar and on top of cuffs, with Bullion Knot and wings with lazy daisy st (see diagram). Embroider heads.

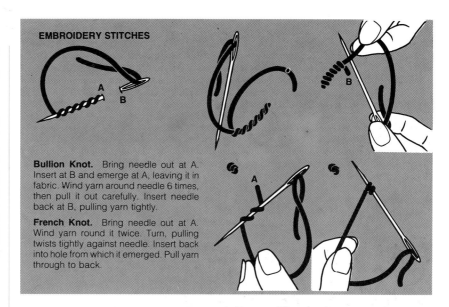

EMBROIDERY STITCHES

Bullion Knot. Bring needle out at A. Insert at B and emerge at A, leaving it in fabric. Wind yarn around needle 6 times, then pull it out carefully. Insert needle back at B, pulling yarn tightly.

French Knot. Bring needle out at A. Wind yarn round it twice. Turn, pulling twists tightly against needle. Insert back into hole from which it emerged. Pull yarn through to back.

Bootees

Using main colour throughout, work as Bootees of Striped Sweater with Zigzag Collar, omitting edging. Work picot edging around front edge of bootees as given for Right Front Band of Cardigan. Embroider bees on top of each bootee as given for Cardigan.

Beanie Hat

With 3¼ mm (No 10/US 3) needles, cast on 115 sts.
1st row P1, [K1, P1] to end.
2nd row K1, [P1, K1] to end.
Rep these 2 rows until work measures 14 cm/5½ in from beg.
Shape top
Dec row Rib 2, [work 3 tog, rib 3] 18 times, work 3 tog, rib 2. Work 3 rows straight.

Dec row Rib 1, [work 3 tog, rib 1] 19 times.
Dec row Rib 1, [work 2 tog] to end. 20 sts. Break off yarn, thread end through rem sts, pull up and secure, then join seam, reversing seam at lower edge to allow for turning.

Feelers (make 2)
With 3¼ mm (No 10/US 3) needles, cast on 7 sts. Work 6 cm/2¼ in in st st. Cast off. Roll lengthwise and slip stitch outside edge. Sew to top of hat.

Fisherman's Rib Sweater with Saddle Shoulders

SEE PAGE
35

MATERIALS

4 (5:5) 100g balls of Hayfield Brig Aran or 3 (4:4) 100g balls of Hayfield Grampian Aran.
1 pair each of 3¾ mm (No 9/US 4) and 4½ mm (No 7/US 6) knitting needles.
Set of four 3¾ mm (No 9/US 4) double pointed knitting needles.

MEASUREMENTS

To fit age
12 (18:24) months
All round at chest
65 (69:73) cm 25½ (27:28¾) in
Length to shoulder
35 (38:41) cm 13¾ (15:16) in
Sleeve seam
21 (23:25) cm 8¼ (9:10) in

TENSION

20 sts and 38 rows to 10 cm/4 in over rib patt on 4½ mm (No 7/US 6) needles.

ABBREVIATIONS

K1b = knit into next st 1 row below.
Also see page 39.

Back & Front Alike

With 3¾ mm (No 9/US 4) needles, cast on 65 (69:73) sts.
1st row (right side) K1, [P1, K1] to end.
2nd row P1, [K1, P1] to end.
Rep these 2 rows until work measures 4 cm/1½ in from beg, ending with a wrong side row.
Change to 4½ mm (No 7/US 6) needles. Work in patt as follows:
1st row (right side) Slip 1, K to end.
2nd row Slip 1, [K1b, P1] to end.
These 2 rows form rib patt. Cont in rib patt until work measures 31 (34:37) cm/12¼ (13½:14½) in from beg, ending with a wrong side row.
Shape shoulders
Cast off in rib 20 (21:22) sts at beg of next 2 rows. Leave rem 25 (27:29) sts on a holder.

Sleeves

With 3¾ mm (No 9/US 4) needles, cast on 35 (37:39) sts. Work in rib as given for Back for 4 cm/1½ in, ending with a wrong side row.
Change to 4½ mm (No 7/US 6) needles.

Work in rib patt as given for Back, *at the same time*, inc one st at each end of 5th and every foll 4th row until there are 57 (63:67) sts, working inc sts into rib patt. Cont without shaping until work measures 21 (23:25) cm/8¼ (9:10) in from beg, ending with a wrong side row.
Shape saddle
Cast off in rib 20 (23:25) sts at beg of next 2 rows. Mark each end of last row.
Cont without shaping on rem 17 sts for saddle for 10.5 (11:11.5) cm/4 (4¼:4½) in, ending with a wrong side row. Mark each end of last row. Leave these sts on a holder.

Neckband

Sew on sleeves, sewing saddles between markers to cast off sts of Back and Front. With set of four 3¾ mm (No 9/US 4) needles, right side facing and beg at left back saddle, work in rib across left saddle, front neck, right saddle and back neck. 84 (88:92) sts. Work in rounds and rib for 6 cm/2¼ in. Cast off loosely in rib.

To Make Up

Join side and sleeve seams.

Fisherman's Rib Cardigan with Saddle Shoulders

SEE PAGE
34

MATERIALS

5 (6:6) 100g balls of Hayfield Brig Aran or 4 (5:5) 100g balls of Hayfield Grampian Aran.
1 pair each of 3¾ mm (No 9/US 4) and 4½ mm (No 7/US 6) knitting needles.
6 buttons.

MEASUREMENTS

To fit age
    18 (24:36) months
All round at chest
    70 (74:78) cm   27½ (29:30¾) in
Length to shoulder
    38 (41:46) cm   15 (16:18) in
Sleeve seam (with cuff turned back)
    20 (22:25) cm   8 (8½:10) in

TENSION

20 sts and 38 rows to 10 cm/4 in over rib patt on 4½ mm (No 7/US 6) needles.

ABBREVIATIONS

K1b = knit into next st 1 row below.
Also see page 39.

Back

With 3¾ mm (No 9/US 4) needles, cast on 69 (73:77) sts.
1st row (right side) K1, [P1, K1] to end.
2nd row P1, [K1, P1] to end.
Rep these 2 rows until work measures 3 cm/1¼ in from beg, ending with a wrong side row.
Change to 4½ mm (No 7/US 6) needles. Work in patt as follows:
1st row (right side) Slip 1, K to end.
2nd row Slip 1, [K1b, P1] to end.
These 2 rows form rib patt**. Cont in rib patt until work measures 34 (37:42) cm/13½ (14½:16½) in from beg, ending with a wrong side row.
Shape shoulders
Cast off in rib 11 (11:12) sts at beg of next 2 rows and 11 (12:12) sts at beg of foll 2 rows.

Leave rem 25 (27:29) sts on a holder.

Pocket Lining (Make 2)

With 4½ mm (No 7/US 6) needles, cast on 14 (16:16) sts.
Work in st st for 5 cm/2 in, ending with a P row and dec one st at centre of last row. 13 (15:15) sts. Leave these sts on a holder.

Left Front

With 3¾ mm (No 9/US 4) needles, cast on 33 (35:37) sts.
Work as given for Back to **. Cont in rib patt until work measures 8 cm/3 in from beg, ending with a wrong side row.
Place pocket
Next row Patt 13, slip next 13 (15:15) sts onto a holder, patt across sts of one pocket lining, patt to end.
Cont in patt until work measures 19 (22: 25) cm/7½ (8¾:10) in from beg, ending with a wrong side row.
Front shaping
Keeping patt correct, dec one st at end (front edge) of next and at the same edge on every foll 5th (4th:4th) row until 22 (23:24) sts rem.
Cont without shaping until work measures same as Back to shoulder shaping, ending with a wrong side row.
Shape shoulder
Cast off in rib 11 (11:12) sts at beg of next row. Patt 1 row. Cast off rem 11 (12:12) sts.

Right Front

Work as given for Left Front, reversing all shaping and placing pocket as follows:
Next row Patt 7 (7:9), slip next 13 (15:15) sts onto a holder, patt across sts of one pocket lining, patt to end.

Sleeves

With 3¾ mm (No 9/US 4) needles, cast on 35 (37:39) sts.

Work as given for Back to **.
Cont in rib patt, inc one st at each end of 7th and every foll 3rd (3rd:4th) row until there are 65 (69:73) sts, working inc sts into patt.
Cont without shaping until work measures 23 (25:28) cm/9 (10:11) in from beg, ending with a wrong side row.
Shape saddle
Cast off 24 (26:28) sts at beg of next 2 rows. Mark each end of last row.
Cont without shaping on rem 17 sts for saddle for 11 (11.5:12) cm/4¼ (4½:4¾) in, ending with a wrong side row. Mark each end of last row. Leave these sts on a holder.

Front Band

Sew on sleeves, sewing saddles between markers to cast off sts of Back and Fronts. With 3¾ mm (No 9/US 4) needles and right side facing, pick up and K 45 (50:57) sts evenly along straight edge of Right Front, 40 (40:44) sts up shaped edge, rib across right saddle, back neck and left saddle, pick up and K 40 (40:44) sts down shaped edge of Left Front, then 45 (50:57) sts down straight edge of Left Front. 229 (241:265) sts. Beg with a 2nd row, work 2 rows in rib as given for Back.
1st buttonhole row : Rib to last 45 (50:55) sts, [cast off 2, rib 5 (6:7) sts more] 5 times, cast off 2, rib to end.
2nd buttonhole row : Rib to end, casting on 2 sts over those cast off in previous row. Rib 3 rows. Cast off in rib.

Pocket Tops

With 3¾ mm (No 9/US 4) needles and right side facing, rib across sts of one pocket top. Rib 6 rows. Cast off in rib.

To Make Up

Join side and sleeve seams. Catch down pocket linings and sides of pocket edgings. Sew on buttons.

Aran Jackets

SEE PAGE
36-37

MATERIALS

Jacket with Collar : 6 (6:7) 50g balls of Hayfield Pure Wool Classics DK.
1 pair each of 3¼ mm (No 10/US 3) and 4 mm (No 8/US 5) knitting needles.
One 3¼ mm (No 10/US 3) circular needle.
Cable needle.
4 buttons.
Jacket with Hood : 8 (9:10) 50g balls of Hayfield Pure Wool Classics DK.
1 pair each of 3¼ mm (No 10/US 3) and 4 mm (No 8/US 5) knitting needles.

Cable needle.
5 buttons.

MEASUREMENTS

To fit age
    1 (2:3) years
All round at chest
    72 (80:86) cm   28¼ (31½:34) in
Length to shoulder
    32 (35:40) cm   12½ (13¾:15¾) in
Sleeve seam
    21 (22:24) cm   8¼ (8¾:9½) in

TENSION

22 sts and 28 rows to 10 cm/4 in over st st on 4 mm (No 8/US 5) needles.

ABBREVIATIONS

C4B = sl next 2 sts onto cable needle and leave at back, K2, then K2 from cable needle.
C4F = sl next 2 sts onto cable needle and leave at front, K2, then K2 from cable needle.
CB = sl next st onto cable needle and

leave at back, K2, then P1 from cable needle.
CF = sl next 2 sts onto cable needle and leave at front, P1, then K2 from cable needle.
Also see page 39.

Panel A – worked over 10 sts.
1st row and 3 foll alt rows (wrong side) K1, P8, K1.
2nd row P1, C4B, C4F, P1.
4th row P1, K8, P1.
6th row P1, C4F, C4B, P1.
8th row As 4th row.
These 8 rows form patt.

Panel B – worked over 15 sts.
1st row (wrong side) K5, P2, K1, P2, K5.
2nd row P5, slip next 3 sts onto cable needle and leave at back, K2, now slip first (P) st from cable needle back onto left hand needle and P it, then K2 from cable needle, P5.
3rd row and every alt row K the K sts and P the P sts as they appear.
4th row P4, CB, K1, CF, P4.
6th row P3, CB, K1, P1, K1, CF, P3.
8th row P2, CB, K1, [P1, K1] twice, CF, P2.
10th row P1, CB, K1, [P1, K1] 3 times, CF, P1.
12th row P1, CF, P1, [K1, P1] 3 times, CB, P1.
14th row P2, CF, P1, [K1, P1] twice, CB, P2.
16th row P3, CF, P1, K1, P1, CB, P3.
18th row P4, CF, P1, CB, P4.
20th row As 2nd row.
22nd row P4, CB, P1, CF, P4.
24th row P3, CB, P3, CF, P3.
26th row P3, K2, P2, [K1, P1, K1, P1, K1] all in next st, turn, P5, turn, K5, turn, P2 tog, P1, P2 tog, turn, slip 1, K2 tog, psso, P2, K2, P3.
28th row P3, CF, P3, CB, P3.
30th row P4, CF, P1, CB, P4.
These 30 rows form patt.

Jacket with Collar

Back
With 3¼ mm (No 10/US 3) needles, cast on 95 (101:107) sts.
1st row (right side) K1, [P1, K1] to end.
2nd row P1, [K1, P1] to end.
Rep these 2 rows until work measures 4 cm/1½ in from beg, ending with a wrong side row.
Next row Rib 3 (2:1), [inc in next st, rib 3] to last 4 (3:2) sts, inc in next st, rib to end. 118 (126:134) sts.
Change to 4 mm (No 8/US 5) needles.
Work in patt as follows:
1st row (wrong side) K1 [P1, K1] 3 (5:7) times, *K1, P4, K1, work 1st row of Panels A, B and A, K1, P4, K1*, work 1st row of Panel A, rep from * to * once, K1, [P1, K1] 3 (5:7) times.
2nd row P1, [K1, P1] 3 (5:7) times, *P1, K4, P1, work 2nd row of Panels A, B and A, P1, K4, P1*, work 2nd row of Panel A, rep from * to * once, P1, [K1, P1] 3 (5:7) times.
3rd row P1, [K1, P1] 3 (5:7) times,* K1, P4, K1, work 3rd row of Panels A, B and A, K1, P4, K1*, work 3rd row of Panel A, rep from * to * once, P1, [K1, P1] 3 (5:7) times.

4th row K1, [P1, K1] 3 (5:7) times,* P1, C4F, P1, work 4th row of Panels A, B and A, P1, C4B, P1*, work 4th row of Panel A, rep from * to * once, K1, [P1, K1] 3 (5:7) times.
These 4 rows set patt. Cont in patt as set, working appropriate rows of Panels until work measures 32 (35:40) cm/12½ (13¾: 15¾) in from beg, ending with a wrong side row.
Shape shoulders
Cast off 19 (20:21) sts at beg of next 2 rows and 18 (20:22) sts at beg of foll 2 rows.
Leave rem 44 (46:48) sts on a holder.

Left Front
With 3¼ mm (No 10/US 3) needles, cast on 45 (49:51) sts.
Work in rib as given for Back until work measures 4 cm/1½ in from beg, ending with a wrong side row.
Next row Rib 4 (6:3), [inc in next st, rib 3] to last 1 (3:0) sts, rib 1 (3:0). 55 (59:63) sts.
Change to 4 mm (No 8/US 5) needles.
Work in patt as follows:
1st row (wrong side) K2, P4, K1, work 1st row of Panels A, B and A, K1, P4, K2, [P1, K1] 3 (5:7) times.
2nd row [P1, K1] 3 (5:7) times, P2, K4, P1, work 2nd row of Panels A, B and A, P1, K4, P2.
3rd row K2, P4, K1, work 3rd row of Panels A, B and A, K1, P4, K1, P1, [K1, P1] 3 (5:7) times.
4th row K1, [P1, K1] 3 (5:7) times, P1, C4F, P1, work 4th row of Panels A, B and A, P1, C4B, P2.
These 4 rows set patt.** Cont in patt as set, working appropriate rows of Panels until work measures 20 (22:25) cm/8 (8¾:10) in, from beg, ending with a wrong side row.
Shape neck
Keeping patt correct, dec one st at end (neck edge) on next row and at same time on foll 4 rows, then on every foll alt row until 37 (40:43) sts rem.
Cont without shaping for a few rows until work measures same as Back to shoulder shaping, ending with a wrong side row.
Shape shoulder
Cast off 19 (20:21) sts at beg of next row.
Work 1 row. Cast off rem 18 (20:22) sts.

Right Front
Work as given for Left Front, reversing position of double moss st (side edge) patt and all shaping.

Sleeves
With 3¼ mm (No 10/US 3) needles, cast on 41 (45:49) sts.
Work in rib as given for Back until work measures 4 cm/1½ in from beg, ending with a wrong side row.
Next row Rib 3 (5:7), [inc in each of next 2 sts, rib 1] to last 2 (4:6) sts, rib to end. 65 (69:73) sts.
Change to 4 mm (No 8/US 5) needles.
Work in patt as follows:
1st row (wrong side) [K1, P1] 4 (5:6) times, K2, P4, K1, work 1st row of Panels A, B and A, K1, P4, K2, [P1, K1] 4 (5:6) times.
2nd row [P1, K1] 4 (5:6) times, P2, K4, P1, work 2nd row of Panels A, B and A, P1, K4, P2, [K1, P1] 4 (5:6) times.

3rd row P1, [K1, P1] 4 (5:6) times, K1, P4, K1, work 3rd row of Panels A, B and A, K1, P4, K1, P1, [K1, P1] 4 (5:6) times.
4th row K1, [P1, K1] 4 (5:6) times, P1, C4F, P1, work 4th row of Panels A, B and A, P1, C4B, P1, K1, [P1, K1] 4 (5:6) times.
These 4 rows set patt. Cont in patt as set, working appropriate rows of Panels, at the same time, inc one st at each end of next and every foll 5th (5th:6th) row until there are 79 (83:87) sts, working inc sts into double moss st (side edge) patt.
Cont without shaping until work measures 21 (22:24) cm/8¼ (8¾:9½) in from beg, ending with a wrong side row. Cast off.

Front Bands and Collar
Join shoulder seams.
With 3¼ mm (No 10/US 3) circular needle and right side facing, pick up and K 48 (52:58) sts up straight edge of Right Front to neck shaping, 44 (46:50) sts along shaped edge to shoulder, K 44 (46:48) sts across back neck inc one st at centre, pick up and K 44 (46:50) sts down shaped edge of Left Front and 48 (52:58) sts along straight edge to cast on edge. 229 (243:265) sts.
Work backwards and forwards in rib as given for Back. Rib 1 row.
Shape collar
Next row Rib to last 84 (88:98) sts, turn.
Next row Sl 1, rib to last 84 (88:98) sts, turn.
Next 2 rows Sl 1, rib to last 80 (84:94) sts, turn.
Next 2 rows Sl 1, rib to last 76 (80:90) sts, turn.
Cont in this way, working 4 more sts at end of every row until the 2 rows of "sl 1, rib to last 48 (52:58) sts, turn" have been worked.
Next row Sl 1, rib to end.
Rib 3 rows across all sts.
1st buttonhole row Rib 4, [cast off 2, rib 11 (12:14) sts more] 4 times, rib to end.
2nd buttonhole row Rib to end, casting on 2 sts over those cast off in previous row.
Rib 4 rows. Cast off in rib.

To Make Up
Sew on sleeves, placing centre of sleeves to shoulder seams. Join side and sleeve seams. Sew on buttons.

Jacket with Hood

Back
Work as given for Back of Jacket with Collar, but cast off sts on back neck.

Left Front
Work as given for Left Front of Jacket with Collar to **.
Cont in patt as set, working appropriate rows of Panels until work measures 27 (30:35) cm/10½ (11¾:13¾) in from beg, ending with a right side row.
Shape neck
Cast off 8 sts at beg of next row. Dec one st at neck edge on every row until 37 (40:43) sts rem. Complete as given for Left Front of Jacket with Collar.

continued overleaf

Right Front

Work as given for Left Front, reversing position of double moss st (side edge) patt and all shaping.

Sleeves

Work as given for Sleeves of Jacket with Collar.

Buttonhole Band

With 3¼ mm (No 10/US 3) needles and right side facing, pick up and K 77 (85:93) sts evenly along straight edge of Left Front. Work 3 rows in rib as given for Back of Jacket with Collar.
1st buttonhole row Rib 3, [cast off 2, rib 14 (16:18) sts more] 4 times, cast off 2, rib to end.
2nd buttonhole row Rib to end, casting on 2

sts over those cast off in previous row. Rib 4 rows. Cast off in rib.

Button Band

Work to match Buttonhole Band, omitting buttonholes.

Hood

With 3¼ mm (No 10/US 3) needles, cast on 37 (39:41) sts.
Next row K1 (4:3), [K twice in next st, K1] to last 0 (3:2) sts, K 0 (3:2). 55 (55:59) sts.
Change to 4 mm (No 8/US 5) needles.
Work in patt as given for 1st (1st:2nd) sizes on Left Front, work 3 rows.
Cont in patt and inc one st at beg of next row and 7 foll 6th rows, working inc sts into double moss st patt. 63 (63:67) sts. Patt 49 rows straight. Dec one st at beg of next and

7 foll 6th rows. Patt 3 rows straight. 55 (55:59) sts.
Change to 3¼ mm (No 10/US 3) needles.
Next row K1 (4:3), [K2 tog, K1] to last 0 (3:2) sts, K0 (3:2). 37 (39:41) sts. Cast off.

Hood Edging

With 3¼ mm (No 10/US 3) needles and right side facing, pick up and K 127 sts evenly along long straight edge of Hood. Work 5 rows in rib as given for Back of Jacket with Collar. Cast off in rib.

To Make Up

Join shoulder seams. Sew on sleeves, placing centre of sleeves to shoulder seams. Join side and sleeve seams. Fold hood in half and join back seam. Sew in place. Sew on buttons.

Guernsey Style Sweater

SEE PAGE
38

MATERIALS

6 × 50g balls of Hayfield Silky Cotton DK.
1 pair each of 3¼ mm (No 10/US 3) and 4 mm (No 8/US 5) knitting needles.
Set of four 3¼ mm (No 10/US 3) double pointed knitting needles.
Cable needle.

MEASUREMENTS

To fit age   2 (3) years
All round at chest
                64 (70) cm   25¼ (27½) in
Length to shoulder
                40 (47) cm   15¾ (18½) in
Sleeve seam 20 (24) cm   8 (9½) in

TENSION

22 sts and 28 rows to 10 cm/4 in over st st on 4 mm (No 8/US 5) needles.

ABBREVIATIONS

See page 39.

Panel A – worked over 6 sts.
1st row (right side) K6.
2nd row P6.
3rd row Slip next 3 sts onto cable needle and leave at front, K3, then K3 from cable needle.
4th row P6.
5th to 8th rows Rep 1st and 2nd rows twice.
These 8 rows form patt.

Panel B – worked over 15 sts.
1st row (right side) K15.
2nd row P15.
3rd row K7, P1, K7.
4th row P6, K1, P1, K1, P6.
5th row K5, P1, [K1, P1] twice, K5.
6th row P4, K1, [P1, K1] 3 times, P4.
7th row K3, P1, [K1, P1] 4 times, K3.
8th row P2, K1, [P1, K1] 5 times, P2.
9th row As 7th row.
10th row As 6th row.
11th row As 5th row.

12th row As 4th row.
13th row As 3rd row.
14th row P15.
These 14 rows form patt.

Back

With 3¼ mm (No 10/US 3) needles, cast on 75 (79) sts.
1st row [K2, P2] to last 3 sts, K2, P1.
This one row forms rib patt. Rep this row until work measures 4 (5) cm/1½ (2) in from beg and inc 4 (6) sts evenly across last row. 79 (85) sts.
Change to 4 mm (No 8/US 5) needles.
Work in patt as follows:
1st row (right side) K4 (7), *P1, [K1, P1] 3 times, K2, P2, work 1st row of Panel A, P2, K2, P1, [K1, P1] 3 times*, work 1st row of Panel B, rep from * to * once, K4 (7).
2nd row P4 (7), *[P1, K1] 3 times, P3, K2, work 2nd row of Panel A, K2, P3, [K1, P1] 3 times*, work 2nd row of Panel B, rep from * to * once, P4 (7).
These 2 rows set patt. Cont in patt as set, working appropriate rows of Panels until work measures 40 (47) cm/15¾ (18½) in from beg, ending with a wrong side row.
Shape shoulders
Cast off 13 (14) sts at beg of next 2 rows and 14 (15) sts at beg of foll 2 rows. Leave rem 25 (27) sts on a holder.

Front

Work as given for Back until work measures 36 (42) cm/14¼ (16½) in from beg, ending with a wrong side row.
Shape neck
Next row Patt 34 (36), turn.
Work on this set of sts only.
Keeping patt correct, dec one st at neck edge on every row until 27 (29) sts rem.
Cont without shaping for a few rows until work measures same as Back to shoulder shaping, ending at side edge.

Shape shoulder
Cast off 13 (14) sts at beg of next row. Patt 1 row. Cast off rem 14 (15) sts.
With right side facing, slip first 11 (13) sts onto a holder, rejoin yarn to rem sts and patt to end. Complete to match first side.

Sleeves

With 3¼ mm (No 10/US 3) needles, cast on 35 sts. Work in rib patt as given for Back for 4 (5) cm/1½ (2) in.
Next row Rib 2, [work twice in each of next 2 sts, rib 1] 11 times. 57 sts.
Change to 4 mm (No 8/US 5) needles.
Work in patt as follows:
1st row (right side) *K2, P2, work 1st row of Panel A, P2, K2*, P1, [K1, P1] 3 times, work 1st row of Panel B, P1, [K1, P1] 3 times, rep from * to * once.
2nd row *P2, K2, work 2nd row of Panel A, K2, P2*, P1, [K1, P1] 3 times, work 2nd row of Panel B, P1, [K1, P1] 3 times, rep from * to * once.
These 2 rows set patt. Cont in patt as set, working appropriate rows of Panels, *at the same time*, inc one st at each end of every foll 3rd row until there are 79 (85) sts, working inc st into moss st patt (as panels at each side of Panel B).
Cont without shaping until work measures 20 (24) cm/8 (9½) in from beg, ending with a wrong side row. Cast off.

Collar

Join shoulder seams.
With right side facing, slip first 6 (7) sts from holder at centre front neck onto safety pin, rejoin yarn and using set of four 3¼ mm (No 10/US 3) needles K rem 5 (6) sts, pick up and K 15 (17) sts up right front neck, K across 25 (27) sts at back neck inc one st at centre, pick up and K 15 (17) sts down left front neck then K 2 tog, K 4 (5) sts from safety pin. 66 (74) sts.
Work 6 rounds in K1, P1 rib, dec one st at

end of last round, turn. 65 (73) sts.
Now work backwards and forwards as follows:
Next row K1, [P1, K1] to end.
This row forms moss st.

Next row K1, M1, moss st to last st, M1, K1.
Next row K1, moss st to last st, K1.
Rep last 2 rows until work measures 6 cm/2¼ in from beg of moss st. Cast off loosely in moss st.

To Make Up
Sew on sleeves, placing centre of sleeves to shoulder seams.
Join side and sleeve seams.

Crochet Hat

SEE PAGE
38

MATERIALS
1 (2) 50g balls of Hayfield Silky Cotton DK.
4.00 mm crochet hook

MEASUREMENTS
To fit age   18–24 (24–36) months

TENSION
18 sts and 14 rows to 10cm/4 in over patt.

ABBREVIATIONS
Ch = chain; dc = double crochet; ss = slip stitch; tr = treble.
Also see page 39.

To Make
With crochet hook, make 3 ch, ss into 1st ch to form a ring, ss in first dc.
1st round Work 6 dc into ring, ss in first dc.

2nd round [2 dc into first st, 1 dc into next st] 3 times, ss into first dc.
3rd round [2 dc into first st, 1 dc into next st] 4 times, 2 dc into next st, ss into first dc.
4th round [2 dc into first st, 2 dc into next st, 1 dc into next st] 4 times, 2 dc into each of next 2 sts, ss into first dc. 24 sts.
5th round 3 ch, 1 tr into last dc of last round, [miss next st, 1 tr into next st, 1 tr into missed st] to end, ss into top of 3 ch.
6th round 1 ch (counts as 1 dc), 1 dc into first st, [2 dc into next st] to end, ss into top of 1 ch. 48 sts.
7th round As 5th round.
8th round 1 ch, 1 dc into first st, 1 dc into each of next 2 sts, 2 dc into next st, [2 dc into next st, 1 dc into each of next 2 sts, 2 dc into next st] to end, ss into top of 1 ch. 72 sts.
9th round As 5th round.

2nd size only
10th round 1 ch, 1 dc into firts st, 1 dc into each of next 4 sts, 2 dc into next st, [2 dc into next st, 1 dc into each of next 4 sts, 2 dc into next st] to end, ss into top of 1 ch. 96 sts.
11th round As 5th round.
Both sizes
Next 2 rounds 1 ch, 1 dc into each st to end, ss into top of 1 ch.
Next round As 5th round.
Next round 1 ch, 1 dc into each st to end, ss into top of 1 ch.
Rep last 2 rounds 2 (3) times more.
Next round 1 ch, 1 dc into each st to end, ss into top of 1 ch.
Next round 1 dc into first st, [3 ch, ss into 3rd ch from hook (picot made), miss 1 st, 1 dc into next st] to last st, 3 ch, ss into 3rd ch from hook, ss into top of first dec. Fasten off.

Source Guide

For local stockists of Hayfield Yarns in your country, please write to the address below:

AUSTRALIA
Panda Yarns (International) Pty Ltd
314–320 Albert Street, West Brunswick, Victoria 3057.
Tel: (03) 387 4033

CANADA
Estelle Designs & Sales Ltd
Unit 65 & 67, 2220 Midland Avenue, Scarborough, Ontario, M1P 3E6.
Tel: (416) 298 9922

DENMARK
Ove Andersen
Harkaor 32, DK–2730, Herlev.
Tel: (42) 910 074

EGYPT
Bahnasy for Trade
5 El Nasr Street, El Khamisi, Alexandria.
Tel: 203 809 409

GERMANY
Woll-Schulze Gmbh & Co KG
4800 Bielefeld 1, Herforder Strasse 297.
Tel: (521) 78 790

GREAT BRITAIN
Hayfield Textiles Ltd
Hayfield Mills, Glusburn, Keighley, West Yorkshire BD20 8QP.
Tel: (0535) 633 333

HONG KONG
B P Trading Company
Block G, 9th Floor, Hop Hing Industrial Bldg, 702 Castle Peak Road, Kowloon.
Tel: 741 6268

ICELAND
Arval
PO Box 4011, 124 Reykjavik.
Tel: (1) 687 950

JAPAN
Dia Keito Co Ltd
1–5–23 Nakatsu Kita-Ku, Osaka 531.
Tel: 353 48 177

KOREA
Kosell International Inc
CPO Box 9831, Seoul.
Tel: (2) 980 0774

MALAYSIA
Malayan Shoes Machinery SDN BHD
128 Jalan Selar, Taman Bukit Ria, Off Batu 4, Jalan Cheras, 56100 Kuala Lumpur.
Tel: (3) 971 6418

NEW ZEALAND
Katex Enterprises Ltd
Unit 2, Mt Wellington Industrial Park, Allright Place, PO Box 62–2000, Mt Wellington, Auckland.
Tel: (09) 527 3241

NORWAY
Garnglede AS
Sporveisgaten 31, 0354 Oslo 3.
Tel: (2) 606 995

SINGAPORE
Malayan Traders Syndicate Ltd
Maxwell Road, PO Box 929, Singapore 9018.
Tel: 746 6141

SOUTH AFRICA
Chester Mortonson CC
2nd Floor Access City, 32 Staib Street, New Doorn Fontein, Johannesburg 2000.

SWEDEN
Jachi Agenturer
Box 172, 423 22 Torslanda, Gothenburg.
Tel: (31) 92 1156

UNITED STATES OF AMERICA
Cascade Yarns Inc
204 Third Avenue, South Seattle, Washington 98104.
Tel: (206) 628 2960

Author's credits. I would like to thank the following for their generous help: Gisela Blum, Kate Jones, Grace Paull, Debbie Scott, and in particular, Fiona McTague for her creative, practical and moral support.

I am grateful for the invaluable help of the following knitters: Lynda Clarke, Elaine Craig, Miriam Hudson, Kay Murphy and Betty Webb.

I would also like to thank Tina Egleton for her technical expertise and pattern checking; Sandra Lousada for the beautiful photography; Marie Willey for her great styling; and Fiona MacIntyre and Heather Jeeves for making the book possible.

The publishers would like to thank the following for their assistance in the production of this book:
General Clothing Company, The Camberwell Business Centre, 99–103 Lomond Grove, London SE5 7HN, Tel 071 703 1974; The Nursery, 103 Bishops Road, London SW6 7AX, Tel 071 731 6637; Nipper Mail Order, Gloucester House, 45 Gloucester Street, Brighton, East Sussex BN1 4EW, Tel 0273 693 785; Jacardi, 473 Oxford Street, London W1, Tel 071 491 9141; Ravel, all branches c/o Tel 0252 33 4091; Next Boys and Girls, Kensington High Street, London W8; Hennes, all branches, c/o 34–42 Cleveland Street, London W1P 5FB, Tel 071 323 2211; Scotch House, 2 Brompton Road, London SW1.